"Need help with your marriage? In this insightful and solid book, the Stoppes give real help! They put their fingers on problems and attitudes that plague every marriage—and then supply answers, solutions, and counsel from God's Word."

Elizabeth George
bestselling author, *A Woman After God's Own Heart*

"A vast amount of the misery and brokenness people experience is the result of lies they believe. This is certainly true of marriage. Steve & Rhonda Stoppe debunk misleading myths with grace, humor, and candor and leave you with hope that your marriage can become more than the stuff of your dreams: It can be the handiwork of God."

Richard Blackaby, PhD
author, *Customized Parenting in a Trending World*

"If you've ever been through a difficult season in marriage, you may have secretly wondered whether you'd be happier with someone else…In this terrific book, *The Marriage Mentor* walks through several critical areas of discontentment, busts the myths that are so easy to believe, and shows just how important it is to rely on God—and how to do that—in order to move from heartache to joy in your marriage. This is the book for everyone who wants to be content and happy in marriage but may not know how."

Shaunti Feldhahn, social researcher and
bestselling author of *For Women Only*

"I just loved reading *The Marriage Mentor*! Are you searching for the secret to a happy marriage? The Stoppes not only deliver practical steps to finding your happily-ever-after, they share a life-changing message of how to use a Christ-centered marriage for the glory of God."

Erica Galindo, founder, CEO, and editorial director
SonomaChristianHome.com

"*The Marriage Mentor* packs practical wisdom and many 'aha moments' to shed light on the myths that sabotage relationships. Through storytelling, humor, and biblical insights, the Stoppes reveal where true joy originates and the secret of becoming your husband's best friend. Bravo on such a well-written and much-needed message."

Julie Gorman, author of *What I Wish My Mother
Had Told Me About Men*

"I loved this book. Read it only if you dare to be inspired to better your marriage. *The Marriage Mentor* is a must-read for anyone. Steve and Rhonda's love for others shines through every page."

Carmen Whittaker
wife of Fermin Whittaker,
executive director, California Southern Baptist Convention

"If you're finding your happily-ever-after not turning out as expected and being shattered by your not-so-perfect Prince Charming, then Rhonda Stoppe is the fairy godmother who will point you in the right direction for a happy ending made in the kingdom of heaven!"

Angela Rose
founder, TheLaundryMoms.com

"Rhonda and Steve Stoppe have been long-distance pastors and mentors to my wife and me over the past 15 years. They are the most grounded-in-the-Bible people we have ever met. Because of that they have been an amazing example of how God intended a married couple to live as husband and wife, and mother and father."

Josh Berry
president, LabeLive

"Rhonda Stoppe makes me want to be a better wife, a better mother, and a better grandmother. But most of all, Rhonda inspires me to be a better Christian through her own very real and passionate relationship with Jesus."

Joy Lucius
journalist, *American Family Journal*
author, *The Dandelion Trial*

"When my husband had an affair, I thought my marriage was over. But Rhonda and Steve Stoppe helped us begin the healing process in our marriage by covering my husband and me with the love of our Savior. Their personal mentorship has been instrumental in making our heavy circumstances less burdensome, and they provide godly marriage counsel that imparts hope for the future."

Angie
humbled and blessed wife
and student of the Word

THE Marriage MENTOR

Steve and Rhonda Stoppe

HARVEST HOUSE PUBLISHERS
EUGENE, OREGON

Cover by Juicebox Designs

Cover photos © Andy Roberts / Getty Images / Hand-lettering by Kristi Smith

Back cover photo © Jackie Plaza Photography

The Marriage Mentor
Copyright © 2018 Rhonda Stoppe
Published by Harvest House Publishers
Eugene, Oregon 97408
www.harvesthousepublishers.com
ISBN 978-0-7369-7143-0 (pbk.)
ISBN 978-0-7369-7144-7 (eBook)

The Library of Congress has catalogued the previous edition as follows:

Stoppe, Rhonda, 1961-
  If my husband would change, I'd be happy / Rhonda Stoppe.
     pages cm
  ISBN 978-0-7369-6286-5 (pbk.)
  1. Marriage—Religious aspects—Christianity. 2. Husbands—Psychology. I. Title.
  BV835.S8775 2015
  248.8'435—dc23
                    201404348

Printed in the United States of America

18 19 20 21 22 23 24 25 / BP-SK / 10 9 8 7 6 5 4 3 2 1

To my husband, Steve Stoppe,
the love of my life for more than 30 years:
By your example, you have taught me how
to love selflessly and fervently.
You are my Stoppe-Ever-After.
I pray God gives us many more years to serve Him together
in this mission:
To know Christ and make Him known.

To our grandchildren:
Karis, Ivy, Eliza, Ledger, Everly, McKenzie, Kelsey, and William
(and the many more yet to be):
We pray that God draws each of your hearts
to know and love our Savior
and that God one day draws to each of you a godly
spouse who loves Jesus more than life itself.

To our children and their spouses:
Tony and Kylene
Jake and Meredith
Brandon and Jessy
Estevan and Kayla
We are in awe of how your marriages reflect the love of Christ
to a world in desperate need of a Savior.

Soli Deo gloria

Acknowledgments

Thank you, Gayle, Molly, Joan, Elaine, Pam, Penny, and Marge, for becoming the Titus 2 women in my life when I was a young bride. The way you love your husbands drew me to you, and the way you love Christ caused me to want to love Him as well. "I thank my God upon every remembrance of you" (Philippians 1:3).

Special thanks to...

My husband—Steve Stoppe, for partnering with me to write this book. As a pastor, counselor, and husband, your words are insightful and inspiring to me, and to anyone who takes them to heart.

My editors—Kathleen Kerr, for her amazing suggestions and support, and Steve Miller, whose insights and wise counsel have helped Steve and me author this marriage resource for a generation that is desperate to believe a happy marriage can last for a lifetime.

Thank you to each and every one of you who will read and apply the biblical principles in this book, and to those of you who will help us mentor the multitudes by sharing this resource with your friends, churches, small groups, and in your social media. Your sharing helps us help others build a no-regrets marriage.

Contents

~

Introduction 9

1. If Your Spouse Would Change,
   Would You Be Happy? 13

2. What's the Big Deal About Respect? 33

3. We're Falling Out of Love 51

4. Your Marriage Can Survive Toddlers and Teens 67

5. The Grass Is Not Greener on the Other Side 89

6. Telling Her She's Pretty and Keeping His Attention 111

7. All He Wants Is Sex 131

8. Every Couple Fights 151

9. Our Marriage Would Be Better If Bad Things
   Would Stop Happening 171

10. Hope to Be Happy 195

11. Happily-Ever-After Is a Fairy Tale 209

    Appendix: How to Have a Relationship with Jesus 225

    Notes 231

Introduction

If you're like most married couples, you are so busy you rarely read through an entire book. And let's be honest: Statistics prove that men aren't the ones reading marriage help books. So rather than writing a book the wife has to continually nag her husband to sit down and read with her, we've broken the book into sections for the wife to read (written by Rhonda) and *small* sections for husbands to read (written by Steve). Then the two of you can watch a short video online of Steve and Rhonda discussing the main point of each chapter together. (The videos are lighthearted and fun, we promise!)

Imagine if you had a weekly appointment with an older couple who could teach you the secrets to building a happy marriage that will last a lifetime. That's what you'll find as you walk with us through the pages of this book. But life gets in the way, and sometimes the immediate needs will drain you and make you think, *There's always tomorrow to work on making my marriage better.*

The truth is, for most couples tomorrow never comes. In over 30 years of ministry we have witnessed countless couples who intended to work on their marriages but never made the time—only to later regret the years they wasted.

On the other hand, we have also been delighted to watch numerous couples we've counseled flourish. We've seen them take seriously the biblical principles laid out in this book, and their marriages reflect joy and happiness like most couples never come to know.

If you're looking for help for your marriage, we ask you to make a commitment now to keep working your way through this book until you reach the end.

But I'm Not a Reader

Steve and I often meet people who say, "I'd love to read your book, but I'm not a reader." To which we reply, "You read social media all day long, so we've established you're a reader." In an attempt to engage with you as the reader, we have written this easy-to-read book that will feel much like you're interacting with us on social media.

Every chapter is broken down into smaller parts so you don't have to feel overwhelmed by trying to read an entire chapter in one sitting. Keep the book on your nightstand, read one or two subsections at a time, and keep moving forward at a pace that works for you as a couple. We know you'll be glad if you do this.

Man to Man

Gentlemen, in each chapter the section for husbands to read is printed in gray so you can't miss it. And the section is small so you can even take a picture of it with your phone and read it on break at work.

From a Husband's Perspective

Ladies, at the close of each chapter, Steve has written a section for the wives called "From a Husband's Perspective." As you read what he says, you will not only glean a man's perspective but also insights from Steve's many years as a pastor and biblical marriage counselor. Women tell us their husbands are loving what their wives are learning from this section. One husband said to his wife, "That is exactly how I feel. I just never knew how to put it into words."

From a Wife's Perspective

Following Steve's man-to-man discussion with husbands, Rhonda will jump in and give husbands a quick insight from a wife's perspective.

Thinking It Through and Living It Out

At the end of each chapter, you will find discussion questions that will prompt healthy conversations. These will allow you as a couple to study and apply to your marriage the truths you've learned. These questions also work well in a group setting should you decide to lead or participate in a small group study through this book.

Marriage Mentor Videos (Free online)

Finally, at the end of each chapter you will be prompted to visit RhondaStoppe.com/marriage-mentor to watch a video of Steve and Rhonda discussing each chapter. The videos are short, lighthearted, and fun. So pour yourself a cup of coffee and settle in for a lively chat. You'll feel like you're hanging out with friends as we walk you through the biblical principles for marriage outlined in each chapter. The videos of Steve and Rhonda will also be a great resource to show to a small group should you decide to facilitate one.

Now, if you are ready, let's begin this journey together. I expect we all will become great friends as we help you build a marriage with no regrets—and share with you *way* too much information about our personal lives. Enter laughing emoji here—LOL.

1

If Your Spouse Would Change, Would You Be Happy?

THE SECRET TO HAPPILY-EVER-AFTER

My dear friend Vi was married for 42 years to Curt, the love of her life. When I asked Vi to tell me about how she and Curt met, she said, "We were in college, on a choir tour. I played the piano and he was going into music ministry, so we were a good fit." Vi jokingly added, "Although, when you play the piano and you marry a minister, you're never quite sure if he married you for love or because he needed a pianist!"

Throughout their married life, Vi and Curt served the Lord in full-time ministry. Vi often referred to their marriage as a waltz through life divinely choreographed by the Lord. Their waltz came to an end when Curt was diagnosed with cancer at age 68. As his health failed, Vi never left his side.

On the last day of his life, Curt looked at his sweetheart and said, "Vi, am I dying?" To which Vi tearfully responded, "Yes, dear—you are dying."

And then in the joyful spirit Curt so adored, Vi whispered, "Curt, you are going home to see Jesus! What is the first thing you want to say to Him when you see His face?"

13

Curt closed his eyes and smiled as he considered the moment he would stand in the presence of the Lord. And then he looked into Vi's gentle eyes and said, "I am going to thank Him for giving me *you.*"

Every time I tell Vi and Curt's love story at a women's event, tears fall all over the room. I think partly because we all love a happily-ever-after love story, but also I think it is because we as wives long to be the kind of wife to whom our husband on his deathbed would say, "I'm going to thank God for giving me you." Rather than, "Thank God it's over! Jesus says we won't be married in heaven, so I'll wave to you if we pass on the streets of gold."

So how do *you* build a marriage like Vi and Curt's? How do you enjoy a love that lasts through the test of time, a love your children will want to emulate? What's the secret to a happily-ever-after love story your grandkids will one day tell their children about long after you are gone?

I'm glad you asked, because we are going to unpack secrets to help you become the wife you long to be—the wife you meant to be on the day you said, "I do." And along the way your husband is going to hear some insights from my husband. So let's get started, shall we?

～

I love being in love. From the depths of my soul I have had an adoration for my husband that has only grown deeper over the past 30-plus years we have been married. Is this adoration a result of being married to a perfect man? Of course not—even though as a young bride I was convinced all of my happiness would be realized on the day I said, "I do" because my husband had promised to be my happily-ever-after.

On the day of our wedding, I walked down the aisle clutching my father's arm because I was trembling. I could hardly believe the day I had dreamt of was finally upon us! I had spent six months planning our wedding, and by the time we were to say our vows, all I could think of was that I would soon be Mrs. Steven W. Stoppe. (I remember writing my new name over and over again just to establish how I would sign it—did you do that?)

I was so nervous as all eyes turned toward me, the bride, who was wearing the biggest hat-veil thing anyone had ever seen! And then, when my eyes met Steve's, nothing else mattered. It took my breath away to see him looking so incredibly handsome in his white tuxedo. (Big hats for veils and white long-tailed tuxedos were in fashion in the 1980s—so don't judge me!)

As our eyes met, I remember thinking, *I cannot believe I am actually marrying this amazing man. I am going to be the best wife he could ever ask for.* Did you feel that way when you got married?

Steve and I wrote our own wedding vows—a real challenge for my not-so-romantically-inclined guy. But he was a good sport, and he wrote wonderful words promising to love me "as long as God shall give me life"—as Steve so sweetly whispered into my ear that day. As a reminder of our promises to one another, the vows we wrote have hung on a wall in our home ever since that day.

To my delight, for our honeymoon, Steve planned a monthlong trip that included driving to see a number of national parks across the United States. What a thrill it was to have an entire month to enjoy ourselves as husband and wife! (Although I have to admit, the nights that we camped out were a bit challenging when I learned how important it was to be near a restroom after lovemaking—can I get a witness?)

Steve's "Aha Moment"

I'm sure that any illusions of grandeur Steve may have had about me when we got married were dashed during the second week of our honeymoon, while we were in Yellowstone National Park.

After a couple of weeks of travel and a lot of fast food, I had gotten pretty constipated—I'm just keepin' it real. You can imagine how uncomfortable I was whenever it was time to be romantic. So Steve decided to help out his poor bound-up wife by giving me a couple of laxatives—something I had never taken before. He assured me if I took the pills before bedtime, I would have a most satisfying bowel movement in the morning, and all would be well.

At Steve's prompting, I took *two* pills. The next morning nothing happened. So we decided to just enjoy our day at Yellowstone and try again that night by taking some more laxatives.

When we drove into the park, we went straight to see the geyser called Old Faithful. Both Steve and I were excited to watch the hot water erupt out from the crater in the ground. We were impressed by how high the water shot up into the sky—so much so that Steve decided it would look even more impressive to view the spectacle from a higher vantage point.

So up a nearby mountain we hiked. Old Faithful spouts at regular intervals throughout the day, and we calculated that we would be able to reach the top of the mountain just in time to see the geyser shoot forth before dark.

Well, I probably don't even have to tell you what happened next. As we hiked and I was getting exercise, my innards began to make the most horrible gurgling sounds. As a blushing bride, I attempted to keep my husband from hearing the atrocious noise. However, the more we hiked, the clearer it became to me that the little pills, along with my morning coffee, were beginning to do a mighty work in my intestines.

Ashamed, I had to tell Steve what was happening, but I assured him I would be able to make it to the top of the mountain in time to see Old Faithful in action. But a short time later, I began to realize not only would I not be able to make it to the top, I was also in danger of not making it back down in time to find a bathroom before I experienced my own geyser spouting off!

Poor Steve—I know he was torn over what to do. He really wanted to continue the hike. I am sure he secretly evaluated the possibility of letting me make my way back down to the bathroom by myself, but then realized this was one of those "for better or worse" moments in which he had promised to love me just two weeks before.

In the end, we hiked slowly down the mountain. I had to stop several times to compose myself before I could go on. And all the while, Steve was laughing hysterically. I am happy to report I did make it to a restroom in time!

By the time I got out, the sun was setting and the park was about to close. So Steve never did have an opportunity to hike back up that mountain.

When the Honeymoon Is Over

Dating, courtship, and planning the wedding are all glorious experiences for most women. But after the honeymoon, when the wedding gifts are in their proper place and life begins to happen, often the glorious experiences fade into the endless routines of to-do lists, juggling finances, and learning to serve one another. Did this happen to you?

It wasn't long before my weekends became consumed with doing laundry and housework. Gone were the Saturdays before marriage, during which Steve and I would spend an entire day at a park lazing by a river, enjoying one another's company. Even as a newlywed, those carefree days already seemed like a distant memory as I washed the dinner dishes and imagined the river running down my kitchen sink.

I remember one Saturday in particular. I was in the house, defrosting our freezer. (They don't even make refrigerators that don't self-defrost anymore, do they?) As I painstakingly chipped away big chunks of ice, I could hear Steve and his brother, Dan, laughing in the garage. Dan had come over to help Steve work on a project. I should have been grateful for the help, but I found myself resenting that they were having a grand old time together while I was stuck in the house thawing out that miserable refrigerator and doing yet another load of *his* dirty laundry. Steve was a carpenter in those days, so his clothes got exceptionally dirty.

It didn't take long before I was annoyed by how much work was involved with being a wife. Soon resentment began building in my heart toward Steve. Even though I had already seen marriages in my family fall apart from resentment, I found myself falling for the mistake of harboring wrong attitudes.

Family of Origin

How would you describe your parents' marriage? Were they head over heels for each other? Did you have a terrific role model from their marriage or other marriages in your family that were characterized by joy, laughter, and delight? I hope this was true for you. In my own upbringing, it was not. So when I thought about what I wanted in my marriage, I had a long list of what I did *not* want.

However, I soon learned that making a list of what you do *not* want your marriage to become is not an effective way to move toward having the marriage of your dreams.

Steve's mother loved cooking, cleaning, and serving her family. Her own mother had died when she was only eleven, so her greatest joy was that God had allowed her to live long enough to care for her children into adulthood. She flittered around humming hymns as she joyfully worked around the house. And if there was no work *in* the house, she would go outside to do yard work. You can imagine how overwhelmed I became when I realized Steve had similar expectations for the kind of wife I would be.

How did you come up with the ideals for your "dream marriage"? After the wedding, were you surprised to discover that many of your expectations for your marriage didn't come true? Did you assume the fun and carefree experiences you enjoyed while you were dating would continue into married life? I did.

While life cannot always be one fun experience after another, you can definitely have a truly satisfying marriage with a love that grows deeper as time goes on. Key to making this happen is breaking free of the common myths wives believe — myths that make us look for marital happiness in all the wrong places.

The Peanut Butter Toast Dilemma

In the early days of our marriage, I remember how I would assign motives to Steve's actions. For example, he loved to make peanut butter toast. And not just in the morning for breakfast. Steve would make peanut butter toast several times throughout the day. Why I had not noticed this man's obsession with peanut butter toast while we were dating, I'll never know.

It wasn't the peanut butter toast that bothered me, but the crumbs that were left behind *every time* Steve made this concoction. I have this unexplainable abhorrence to finding crumbs on my kitchen counter and floor. Mind you, I am not a spotless housekeeper, but the left-behind crumbs seemed to send me the message that Steve didn't care how hard I worked to keep up the house. Although I didn't mention it to Steve, each time he left crumbs behind I felt insulted and betrayed.

Thinking he was saving me the trouble of washing a plate, Steve would invariably make his toast directly on the countertop—the *countertop*! This would leave so many crumbs it was almost unbearable to me.

For the first few months of our marriage, I just quietly wiped up the crumbs while uttering little manipulative—okay, maybe even passive-aggressive—comments about how much I despised crumbs. Then one day I walked into the kitchen and found the countertop covered in crumbs. I must have gasped audibly because Steve came running into the kitchen to see what was the matter.

I burst into tears and explained to Steve how his leaving crumbs behind made me feel like he didn't respect all the work I did to keep the house nice. The poor guy—he just stood there stunned that I would rant so much over peanut butter toast and crumbs. And he wondered why I would feel so betrayed by something as simple as the fact that he left *a few crumbs on the kitchen counter once in a while*.

This story sounds funny now, but when we were first married, the crumb dilemma truly devastated me. Maybe you can relate.

One of the biggest threats to a happy marriage is when one or both parties have unrealistic expectations of each other.

The Danger of Unrealistic Expectations

One of the biggest threats to a happy marriage is when one or both parties have unrealistic expectations of each other. When those expectations are not realized, you might feel betrayed. And this is when you may begin to believe myths that lead you to have unrealistic or incorrect expectations that do harm to your relationship. In this book, we will shed light on those myths. When my expectations of Steve were not being met, I remember feeling betrayed because I was convinced my happiness would rest in how well he treated me. How self-absorbed I was back then. God used my disillusionment to show me my selfish heart. Have you ever had expectations come crashing down around you when reality set in? How did that experience make you feel? Are you in a similar situation right now? Or maybe you have experienced years of disappointment in your marriage. Whatever the case, let's talk for a moment about how disappointment turns to disillusionment.

You might feel betrayed when you come to realize the man you married is not the man you had perceived him to be. If you have been married for any amount of time, I am sure that by now you have your own secret list of things you wish you could change about your husband.

I find it interesting that frequently the very qualities a woman was attracted to while dating her man often become the rub in their relationship after they are married. For example:

BEFORE MARRIAGE	AFTER MARRIAGE
"I love his spontaneity."	"He's irresponsible."
"We can sit for hours just holding hands."	"He doesn't talk to me."
"He's a hard worker."	"He works too much."
"He is frugal."	"He's a tightwad."

I could go on, but you get the picture.

Are You the Wife You Meant to Be?

Are you the wife you meant to be? It's easy to focus on areas where your husband has not met your expectations, but have you considered your husband may have his own secret list of disappointments about you as well? Rather than dwelling on what you wish your *husband* would change, what if you were to make a list of how *you* have changed after marriage? And instead, work to be the woman your husband had hoped you would be—the wife you meant to be—on the day you said, "I do."

Stop for a moment and evaluate the type of wife you had hoped to be…and the kind of wife you actually are. When your husband looked at your beautiful face as you cascaded down the aisle, what kind of wife did *he* expect you would be? Have you measured up to your own expectations—let alone his?

In more than 30 years of ministry, Steve and I have listened to countless couples reveal how disappointed they were in the person they married. Whenever a wife can persuade her husband to come in for biblical marriage counseling, she often secretly says to herself, "Oh good. Now my husband is going to find out all the ways he needs to change to be a better husband so that *I* can be happy."

Can I let you in on a little secret? Looking to your husband to make you happy is an unfair expectation. And no matter how "perfect" he is, he will never bring you true joy. Because the purpose for which you exist is *not* to find happiness in your marriage relationship—contrary to every fairy tale you ever heard as a little girl.

This is key, so listen closely. You were created to delight in your Creator. God made you to long for intimacy with *Him*—to delight in Him. So any other relationship that you pursue to fill the void only God can fill will always come up short. In the same way, you can never be your husband's source of true joy. That's kind of a relief, isn't it?

What's Their Secret?

Do you know a godly couple who have been married for a long time and are still deeply in love? Doesn't your heart long to have a marriage like theirs? What's their secret?

As you observe such a couple, you may be tempted to say, "Oh, that wife is so lucky to be married to such a wonderful man. I wish my husband were more like him."

Upon closer observation, however, you might be surprised to learn that the secret to their happy marriage isn't related to how "ideal" they are as spouses. Rather, it's because their relationship is grounded in a love that is deeper than their love for each other. A marriage flourishes when both husband and wife love Christ more than any other person in life—including one's own spouse.

In Mark 12:30, Jesus declared that the priority of life is to love God with all of your being—*all* of it. Do you love God like that? As a young Christian, I would have answered, "Yes, of course I love God!" and pointed to my busyness in serving God as evidence of that love. However, every once in a while I would meet someone who straight-up loved Jesus. A person whose life wasn't about *doing* things for God; rather, they *lived to love God* so much that they couldn't help but love others. Have you ever met anyone like that?

You know what kind of people I am talking about. You have to spend only a few minutes with them to realize they have an authentic love deep in their heart for their Savior.

This kind of wholehearted love is available to anyone who has a relationship with God through His Son, Jesus. When you learn to *devote* your heart to loving the Lord, there will be a natural outpouring of God's love spilling out of your heart and onto those around you—especially to your husband. (To learn more about a relationship with God through Jesus, please turn to the article in the appendix of this book, "How to Have a Relationship with Jesus.")

It all comes down to this: the key to having an all-out love for your husband and experiencing fulfillment in your marriage does not lie in how well your husband measures up to your expectations, but in how well you love God.

It is humanly impossible to love selflessly because we are all born with a sin nature that seeks our own good above anyone else's. The only people who are able to love the way Jesus intended are those who have a personal relationship with God through Christ, are filled with the Holy Spirit, and are pursuing a deeper love for the Lord. Because God provides His supernatural love to those who love Him, He offers hope for true love to anyone who would follow Christ. Romans 5:5 says, "God's love has been poured into our hearts through the Holy Spirit who has been given to us" (esv). We will talk more about hope for a happy marriage in chapter 10.

Loving your husband amounts to so much more than your emotions and feelings for him at any given moment. Love is a choice. And

God's love gives you the ability to love your husband even when he doesn't measure up to your expectations. Listen to what the Bible says:

> Above all these put on love, which binds everything together in perfect harmony…Above all, keep loving one another *earnestly*, since love covers a multitude of sins (Colossians 3:14; 1 Peter 4:8 ESV, italics added).

Did you know God loves you in this way? Psalm 139:17-18 says, "How precious also are Your thoughts to me, O God! How great is the sum of them! If I should count them, they would be more in number than the sand."

Are you really taking in what this scripture says? The perfect Creator of heaven and earth makes it a point to think *precious thoughts* toward you—*you*!

Let's be honest: you and I both know that if God wanted to, He could write a long list of all our flaws and the ways we fail Him every day. Yet because of His great love, God says, "I, even I, am He who blots out your transgressions for My own sake; and I will not remember your sins" (Isaiah 43:25).

What kind of love is that? A love that chooses to forget your sins and focus on precious thoughts toward you. I know I do not deserve this kind of love. Do you?

Do you see where I am going with this? If God loves you so overwhelmingly even though you don't measure up to His expectations, and you are called to love others as He loves, then you are to have that same kind of love for your husband.

Your Marriage Is a Light

Jesus said, "By this all will know that you are My disciples, if you have love for one another" (John 13:35). Why do you think Satan works so hard to destroy Christian marriage relationships?

Your genuine love for each other will be a light that tells your children—and a watching world—that knowing the Savior really does make a difference in your lives. Letting this light shine does not happen by accident. In fact, if you make marital love all about your feelings, you will certainly miss the opportunity to shine Christ's light.

When life is hard, your hormones are acting up, the bills pile up, and the kids get sick—this is when the light of God's kind of love has the potential to shine the brightest. Jesus said, "Let your light so shine before men, that they may see your good works and glorify your Father in heaven" (Matthew 5:16).

As a young bride, I was drawn to some happily married couples in our church because their love shone as a bright light to me. As I began to look to more mature couples who seemed to delight in one another, do you know what I found? An untapped resource of wisdom that was exactly what I needed to teach me how to have a happy marriage!

Titus 2:4 instructs older women to teach the younger how to love their husbands. The Greek word translated "love" in this verse is *phileo*, which refers to a friendship love. And that is just what these older women taught me—how to enjoy my husband for who he is, not who I wished he would be. Through these godly mentors, I learned how to become his closest and dearest friend. Isn't that what you want for your marriage?

In writing this book, it is my sincere desire to be a godly mentor woman in your life. Because when you learn the secret of becoming your husband's closest friend, you will become your husband's greatest treasure—and he will become yours as well.

So Much More Than Happily-Ever-After

Happy marriages are one of the greatest tools
God uses to draw unbelievers toward Christ.

The world is longing to see married people who grow more in love over time. When Christian marriages do not exude true love, it hurts the name of Christ. God wants the love between you and your spouse to be a testimony of His love to a watching world, and happy marriages are one of the greatest tools God uses to draw unbelievers toward

Christ. The effect of that testimony begins in your home, especially to your children.

While writing this book I laughed and cried over the love stories we have included. And the truths that I discovered as I researched and studied God's Word have forever changed the way I relate to my husband. I cannot wait to share these stories and insights with you!

From a Husband's Perspective
A Word from Steve

So far Rhonda has outlined for you the premise of this book. As you read it you will learn very important and helpful information to help you become the wife I think you hope to be. You're likely going to get excited to be learning so many great things about building a better marriage. And as you learn, you may get charged up to make some major changes right away in your relationship.

If you are like most wives, you'll likely want to talk with your husband about all that you are learning. And in your zeal, you may expect your husband to get on board and *feel* the same excitement you do. While it's a good thing to be motivated to make changes for the good in your marriage, allow me to give you a little insight from a husband's perspective. At first, your hubby may not share your enthusiasm. If this is the case, please don't be discouraged by his lack of excitement. Realize that we men are unbelievably different animals than our wives. Men are usually slower than women to process what they learn. Please try not to hold it against your man if he takes a while to warm up to an idea—especially when he is faced with making changes.

The Bible instructs wives how best to motivate a husband in spiritual matters. And growing your marriage to be more honoring to Christ is certainly a spiritual matter, wouldn't you agree? Let's look at the apostle Peter's exhortation to wives in 1 Peter 3:1-4 (ESV):

> Likewise, wives, be subject to your own husbands, so that even if some do not obey the word, they may be won *without a word by the conduct of their wives*, when they see your

respectful and pure conduct. Do not let your adorning be external—the braiding of hair and the putting on of gold jewelry, or the clothing you wear—but let your adorning be the hidden person of the heart with the imperishable beauty of a gentle and quiet spirit, which in God's sight is very precious (italics added).

If your husband sees you working through the book yourself and applying the biblical principles to your marriage and sees how God is transforming you, he may be won over without a word. As 1 Peter 3:1-4 suggests, he will see the beauty of your gentle and quiet spirit that God says is precious in His sight.

And to spark your husband's interest, here's a little secret: Wives tell Rhonda that when they read to their husbands what men wished their wives knew about sex from chapter 7, it draws their husband into the book and sparks some pretty great discussions—as you might imagine! So if at first your husband is not interested in working through this book with you, you might want to read to him some tidbits out of chapter 7 just for grins!

Pray

As you work through this book, ask God to show you how He would have you respond to the biblical principles you will learn. If the Spirit convicts you of something, be willing to repent and turn from any sinful actions that are hurting your marriage. And if you're secretly thinking, *I'll change when he changes,* you may want to begin there by asking God to soften your heart and help you obey Him regardless of how your husband responds.

Pray for the Lord to grow in you His selfless love for your husband, a love that draws him toward you and to Christ. (If your husband is not a believer, don't beat him over the head with Scripture; rather, let your respect, holiness, and gentle spirit do the work as you simply pray for God to make him not only interested in learning how to be a better husband but ultimately want to know Christ.)

Together, Rhonda and I are praying that what you and your

husband learn in this book will transform your marriage and start some great conversations about how your marriage can grow stronger. May God bless you as you read this book and apply the life-changing truths you discover.

> Wives, listen to chapter 1 audio "Old Faithful" at
> **RhondaStoppe.com/marriage-mentor**

Man to Man

Hey, guys. I'm sure you are just thrilled that your wife is shoving yet another marriage book under your nose. If you're like me, reading a marriage book isn't at the top of your priority list for an evening at home—or anytime, for that matter! But I'm betting you *do* want a happy marriage, right? So hang in there with me and let's see if we can help you get there.

Think of this book as a time you get to hang out with a couple who has walked ahead of you in this journey of marriage—and they're willing to share with you all the secrets they've learned to help you build a marriage with no regrets. Our goal is to provide a resource where your wife can read all the fun stories and insights in the opening section that Rhonda has written, and then you can read the "CliffsNotes" from me in these short sections I'm writing to you.

With that being said, let's get started. As I read the first chapter, what stood out to me is that Rhonda blames me for her unexpected bathroom needs while we were hiking in Yellowstone! I've heard her tell this story a hundred times before. Why did I just now get that? (You can ask your wife to tell you about the hiking story in this chapter. It's actually pretty funny.) When you got married, you likely had great hopes of what you thought marriage would be like. And you probably had a specific idea of the kind of husband you would be too. Let me ask you: How's that working out for you? Are you the husband you intended to be? Is your marriage all you had hoped it would be?

Your ideal of marriage was probably influenced by your parents' marriage. If it was a good marriage, you likely wanted to emulate it. And if their marriage was difficult or nonexistent, you probably had a list of what you did *not* want your relationship to become.

My idea of marriage was what I had seen modeled by my parents. They had a loving relationship. Rhonda referred to them as Mr. and Mrs. Cleaver. My parents were committed to each other, served one another, and rarely quarreled in front of me or my brother. I can count on one hand the times I experienced any real stress in our home. My parents were older when they had kids, so I think they had worked out a lot of their marital stuff before I came along. When Rhonda and I got married, I figured our marital experience would be like my parents'.

I seriously expected my wife to flitter around the house happily cleaning—keeping it tight and tidy, all the while humming hymns while she worked. (My mom seriously did that.) After we were married, I learned quickly the image I envisioned was not at all consistent with reality. I thought wives *liked* to defrost the freezer. Can you imagine my surprise when my young wife tearfully—more like hysterically—informed me that activity was not really in her wheelhouse?

Time to Grow Up

Before Rhonda and I were married, she was a ton of fun. We would water-ski almost every Friday. During the summer months I would impress my lady with my abilities on the skis. I would dip my shoulder close to the water and throw up a giant rooster tail of water. That action would cause her to squeal with delight.

After we were married, I thought it was time to put away all of the fun adventures and get down to the business of life. I figured it was time to move toward being more responsible and serious about what needed to be done.

I even sold my 1969 Ford Mustang Mach 1 at the prompting of my father, who said, "Son, you're getting married now. It's time to grow up." We used the money from the sale of the car for our honeymoon. The car is now worth over $100,000, so Rhonda gets to tell people I took her on a $100,000 honeymoon! (I'm pretty sure I heard some of you audibly groan at the thought of selling my car. I hear ya!)

The other misconception I had was about who I thought I'd be as a husband. When we were dating, Rhonda was a real chatterbox, and I enjoyed her zeal to share with me *every* single detail about her day. However, after we were married a while, I grew a bit disillusioned by the reality of what life was really like with this young lady who had such a gift for gab. That might be a bit of an understatement; Rhonda wanted to talk to me *constantly*!

Rhonda's less-than-joyful response to housework and such, coupled with me feeling a bit smothered by her need to always be with me and wanting to talk through *everything* that rolled around in her head, led me to respond in ways that revealed what kind of man—what kind of husband—I would become. Basically, I wanted to be the guy who preferred to work in the garage and veg in front of the television at the end of a hard day of work. Maybe you can relate?

For some men, arguing or demanding their way is the natural response to stress. For others, withdrawing is the way to escape a less-than-satisfying marriage. But there *is* a way to make your marriage great! When you learn the basic biblical principles for building an amazing marriage, you'll be surprised at how happy your life can become. I've seen it work hundreds of times, and I know it will work for you too.

What's the Purpose of Your Marriage?

God wants your relationship to bring glory to our Savior. God's plan for you as a husband is to serve and love the woman He has given you.

It's easy to look at your wife and wish she would change,

right? But you cannot change her. You only have control over your own thoughts and actions. The best way to help your wife grow more Christlike in how she interacts with you is to step up to God's plan for husbands. For example, God has ordained for you to be her spiritual leader. How are ya doin' with that?

When you determine to daily draw closer to our Savior through prayer, Bible study, and fellowship with other believers who emulate Christ-honoring marriages, you will begin to become the husband you hoped to be. And you will be equipped to lead your wife to do the same.

If you are struggling with some of these things, stay tuned. Together we may be able to work through some stuff that will put your life, your spiritual life, and your marriage in a direction that will result in a happy marriage that glorifies and exalts our Savior—which is the purpose of life for every believer!

From a Wife's Perspective
A Word from Rhonda

Hey, guys—wanna score some points with your wife? How about you take the initiative to set aside time to watch the video together? It may seem like a little thing to you, but gestures this simple will speak volumes to your wife that you care and are interested in growing your marriage to be the best it can be.

Together, watch chapter 1 video at
RhondaStoppe.com/marriage-mentor

Thinking It Through

Do you remember the first time you laid eyes on each other? Take some together time to remember the story of how you met and fell in love. Sharing your precious memories with one another is a great way to rekindle the romance in your marriage because it can remind you of sweet times when your love was young.

For fun you can watch Steve and Rhonda trying to recall their love story. It was more than 40 years ago, so some of the details may or may not be accurate!

Watch: Real Life Romance Steve & Rhonda at
RhondaStoppe.com/marriage-mentor

What's the Big Deal About Respect?

THE CONCEPT OF UNCONDITIONAL RESPECT

Chuck was raised in a Christian home and was committed to remain a virgin until he wed. When Angie was saved as a teen, she also made a covenant with Christ that she would remain a virgin until marriage.

As young adults, Chuck and Angie met, fell in love, and were married. Not long into their marriage, Angie began to realize something was desperately wrong with their sex life. Angie expected Chuck to regularly want her in the marriage bed, but his desire for her was lacking. Finally, Angie found the reason for their trouble: Chuck had been looking at pornography.

When confronted, Chuck explained to Angie how as a junior high boy he had convinced himself that looking at pornography would keep him from having sex until he married. Chuck told Angie how he fully expected to be able to put away the pornography once they had wed.

Through many tears and Chuck's repentance, Angie forgave her husband, who promised never to view pornography again. Of course, anyone who understands this type of addiction realizes that the battle for victory is long and difficult.

Chuck had asked Angie to be his accountability person, but they both came to realize her attempts to help Chuck would be interpreted by him as disrespect, which would only serve to drive Chuck away from Angie.

Maybe you can relate to Chuck and Angie's situation. Wives whose husbands struggle with pornography find it difficult to show their spouse the respect they likely crave. So what can you do if you find yourself in this plight? Let's look at how Angie handled her struggle.

In my book *Real Life Romance*, you can read Chuck and Angie's entire love story. The following excerpt offers tremendous insight to any couple in a similar situation:

- Chuck sought out a group of godly men to hold him accountable and to talk through the root problem of his addiction. Chuck was relieved to learn he was not alone in his battle and found great support from the men with whom he met.

- Angie had to work through her own feelings of insecurity and betrayal. She had put her trust in Chuck and he had let her down. The secrecy was almost more painful than the actual addiction. But Angie was committed to fight this battle alongside her husband. And fight she did—on her knees. Wrestling to take her thoughts captive whenever she dwelt on her disappointment in her husband was the hardest thing she had ever done, and yet it brought her the sense of peace and strength she needed. She joined women's Bible studies to continue her spiritual growth and sought counsel from other women who had walked a similar path ahead of her.

- Forgiving Chuck was hard, but resenting him was even harder. As Angie pressed in to her love for Christ, He gave her His selfless love for Chuck. And as Chuck allowed God's Spirit to strengthen him in his battle against his addiction, he has seen strides of great victory.

Angie gives this advice to any woman who finds herself in a similar situation: "What helped me was prayer. And humbling myself to realize that whatever sin I am addicted to is equal to Chuck's. And as much as I try to break free of my familiar sinful struggles, Chuck is working to break free from his."[1]

If your husband struggles with viewing pornography, rather than badgering him with the silent treatment, withholding sex, or making manipulative comments to shame him toward change, ask God to help you speak words of courage and affirmation to him.

If your husband is a good man, he likely battles with his own shame after he has once again pleasured himself through pornography. And if he is a believer, the Holy Spirit promises to convict him, which will certainly add to his misery.

Rather than making him feel worse, what if you determined to forgive him "seventy times seven" like Jesus instructs in Matthew 18:22? What if you said to him something like this:

> Honey, I believe in you. I know you are a good man and I know you desire to break free from this stronghold as much as I want you to be free. I want you to know that I have forgiven you, and with God's help I will forgive you as many times as it takes. I am in this battle *with* you, not against you.
>
> I've repented of my resentment toward you so I can pray in God's power for Jesus to help you win this war against the enemy. And I am praying God will lead you to another man who has found victory in Christ over the same addiction.

Learning to show your husband the respect he craves, whether you think he deserves it or not, is vital to a healthy marriage. My husband and I have watched failing marriages be turned around when a wife determines to obey God's mandate to show honor to her husband.

Failing to See the Big Picture

Can you think of a time when you failed to see the big picture of your husband's circumstance? Maybe he spent the day battling giants at work while you were at home holding down the fort. Husbands often feel their wives do not understand the battles they have to face at work on a daily basis. Have you ever considered what your husband deals with? Here are a few possibilities to ponder:

- Holding fast to his integrity in a work environment that says, "The ends justify the means."
- Keeping his eyes from longing after other women.
- Putting up with office politics.
- Worrying that someone younger or smarter is after his job.
- Trying to make enough money to make ends meet.
- Battling physical and emotional fatigue.

Many men spend long hours at their job. For some, their work is labor intensive; for others, it is emotionally exhausting. When Steve worked in construction, he would come home physically spent. I remember watching him jump into our swimming pool after a hot day of working in the sun. Steam would rise from the surface of the water when he got into the pool.

And these days, as a pastor, my husband comes home emotionally tired. He has listened and talked to people all day long. So that I could encourage my husband, I had to learn from him what his day was *really* like and not what I perceived it to be. Then I could discern when to talk to him about important matters or encourage him upon his return home.

Far too often husbands are greeted by their wives with a list of complaints! For example, let's say your husband had an amazing week at work. Maybe he is in sales, and after many business meetings and hours of presentations, he lands the biggest account ever. On Friday, the boss calls all the staff together to honor your husband's efforts and thank him for a job well done.

During the drive home, your husband is singing his heart out worshipping the Lord for His favor. He stops to buy a bucket of chicken for dinner and some flowers to give you when he arrives.

All the while, you are at home watching the clock. *Where could he be?* you think to yourself. *He's an hour late.*

When your husband finally pulls into the driveway, you meet him at the door. In a condescending tone, you say, "Where have you been? You are late."

He starts to explain, and when you see the bucket of chicken, you exclaim, "Chicken, seriously? You bought chicken? You could have called, you know. I already made spaghetti. We are having spaghetti tonight. You can take that chicken to work with you for lunch…if you're not already scheduled to have some wonderful business lunches next week while I eat peanut butter and jelly with the kids, *again.*"

As you walk back into the house, you growl over your shoulder, "By the way, you forgot to put the garbage cans away last night. They're still out on the street. Can you go get them now, please? It embarrasses me when you leave the cans out there. Our neighbors must think you are lazy."

After bringing in the garbage cans, your husband places the bouquet of flowers on the kitchen table. To which you respond, "Flowers? I hope you're not expecting to get lucky tonight. I'm exhausted!"

I know *you* would never be the woman in this scenario, but maybe you can relate to a similar rendition of the story. Is it any wonder husbands arrive home from work, grab the remote, and sit in front of the television until it's time to go to sleep?

When it comes to your husband, are you failing to see the big picture and note all he does to provide for your family? Are you preoccupied with his shortcomings, or do you honor his efforts and celebrate his successes and offer him unconditional respect at home in spite of his failures?

When Your Reputation Becomes More Important

My husband was a youth pastor for 18 years, and we both dearly loved all that came with that job. After that, Steve accepted a position as senior pastor of a church. Shepherding adults is certainly different from pastoring teens. I soon discovered women in the church would come to me, rather than my husband, when they had a complaint. Or they would say things to me like, "Can you have your husband call my husband? He is really under a lot of stress at work and needs some encouragement."

It didn't take long for me to develop a habit of telling my husband, "You *need* to call so-and-so because his wife said he is struggling."

What I soon discovered was that Steve would become very quiet and withdrawn when I made these types of comments. One day, as I was asking him if he had yet made the encouraging phone call, I had an "aha moment."

When Steve offered no reason why he had not followed up with the man, I pressed him to do so, adding, "I don't want Mrs. Smith to think I forgot to tell you about her husband."

As I was speaking, the Lord opened my understanding. By agreeing to deliver Mrs. Smith's message to my husband, I was now part of the equation. I didn't want to look bad and have her think I had forgotten to pass along her request. And I didn't want her to think—or tell others—that my husband was uncaring about their situation. I was concerned about my reputation—and ours.

I then asked Steve, "Honey, when I say you *need* to call this person, are you interpreting that as me telling you how to do your job?"

I could see the relief come across Steve's face. The poor guy had been trying to endure my "helpfulness" with a good attitude. Yet each time I would press him to make a contact, all he heard was, "Hey, buddy, I know you're the pastor, but I am here to help you do your job right. If you drop the ball, not only do you look bad as a pastor, but I look bad to these women who are asking me to get you to call their husbands."

In a moment everything changed! I came to realize how much my husband valued my respect. And in this new, uncharted territory of Minister's Wife, I was coming across more concerned about my own reputation and how Steve would be perceived by the women of the church than I was about trusting in Steve's leadership as a pastor.

I quickly asked Steve to forgive me for being disrespectful. I assured him that I trusted his leadership and knew he was seeking the Lord daily for direction. I promised Steve from that day forward, "When women come to me with a request or question, I will tell them they need to talk directly to you—the pastor."

That was almost 20 years ago. And I am so thankful the realization came early on so I did not develop a habit of disrespecting my husband under the impression I was helping him do his job better. Along with this adjustment, I also determined not to correct him in public, talk over him in a meeting, or undermine his authority behind his back. The women of our church have a great respect for my husband because he is a godly leader—and I believe, in part, it is also because they have seen my example of respecting him as the spiritual leader of our body.

Love and Respect

Women long to be loved by their husbands. In all the years my husband and I have done biblical marriage counseling, we have seen that wives are often plagued with the question, "Does he love me as much as I love him?"

For the most part, women ache to know their husbands love them unconditionally. God created women to have this longing, which is why He instructed men, "Husbands, love your wives, just as Christ also loved the church and gave Himself for her" (Ephesians 5:25).

Over the years, I have learned to make myself vulnerable in asking Steve to help me feel loved by him. You may think this sounds needy—okay, call me needy. But I know how much I value being loved by my man, and I am willing to ask him from time to time to show me his love.

The Bible calls husbands to "live with your wives in an understanding way" (1 Peter 3:7 NASB). But let's be honest, ladies—we are a mystery. We aren't even sure what we want much of the time. Based on your hormones and many other variables, actions that say "I love you" today may not be what you need tomorrow. If your husband is going to live with you in an understanding way, it is your responsibility to gently coach him—for the rest of your life—how he can best show you his love.

For example, when I was younger I really appreciated my husband's compliments about my appearance. If he failed to notice when I made an extra effort to look good, rather than hinting or pouting until he noticed, I would say, "Hey, did you notice my new dress/hairstyle/etc.?" When he responded with a compliment, I did not allow myself to think, *Oh yeah, now you say something, buddy. Maybe I'll stop making the effort, and then we'll see how long it takes you to notice.* I'm sure you'll agree that response would be petty, but over the years that I have mentored women I've seen that kind of attitude surface frequently.

Now that I am older, I tell my husband how much more I need his kind affirmation. We joke about how merciful God is to cause our vision to diminish as we age so we see each other through blurred lenses that help to soften all our wrinkles.

And Just as Much As You Need to Feel Loved...

Just as deeply as wives long to be loved without condition, husbands desire to receive unconditional respect from their wives. Again, God knew women did not need to be told to love their man—this comes naturally. But to respect him is another story. That's why the Bible instructs, "Let the wife see that she respects her husband" (Ephesians 5:33 ESV).

Women tend to nurture and mother the people they care about. But your husband does not need a mom. He wants a wife who believes in him, relies on him, and celebrates his accomplishments.

When a man feels disrespected by his wife, he tends to pull away and not show her the love she craves. And when a woman does not feel loved, she will respond by disrespecting her husband. In his book *Love and Respect*, Dr. Emerson Eggerichs calls this the "Crazy Cycle." He says, "The Love and Respect Connection is the key to any problem in a marriage...How the need for love and the need for respect play off of one another in a marriage has *everything* to do with the kind of marriage you will have."[2]

But He Doesn't Deserve My Respect

I completely understand a woman's resistance to showing respect to a man who has not earned it. We already talked about how hard it is for a wife to respect her husband if he regularly looks at pornography.

But just as God instructs a husband to love his wife whether she earns his love or not, God commands a wife to show respect to her husband without condition. Let's consider Dr. Eggerichs's insight into this matter:

> A wife faces two choices. She can try to make personal adjustments and treat her husband respectfully according to what Scripture says, or she can continue with a sour look, and a negative, disrespectful attitude…To continue with disrespect only means shooting herself in both feet.[3]

Learning to show your husband respect is vital to a healthy marriage. My husband and I have watched failing marriages be turned around when a wife determines to obey God's mandate to show respect to her husband.

Are you worried that if you show respect, your husband will "get his way" when conflict arises? Or are you afraid your respectful manner will lessen your chances of motivating your husband to change? Listen to one woman's response to this: "If I step out in faith, claiming God's Word as the basis for my action, then I am trusting God to bring to pass what He said He would do. I can't go wrong with that! I've determined that is the path I am going to take no matter how unfamiliar it seems."[4]

Your respect will motivate your husband to attempt feats he might otherwise only dream about—because a man respected by his woman can accomplish great things!

According to God's Word, showing respect to your husband is not optional. As you spend time in the Bible, ask God to help you focus on and express to your husband what you respect about him. And when you do, don't be surprised if your husband responds in a more loving manner. Because your husband *needs* to be respected by you, when you bless him with honor, he will come to view you as a treasure. And you will become your husband's closest confidant, friend, and encourager. Your respect will motivate your husband to attempt feats he might otherwise only dream about—because a man respected by his woman can accomplish great things!

From a Husband's Perspective
A Word from Steve

To be respected is probably one of the most important needs your husband has. In general, men crave respect. With the promise of respect, gangs seduce young boys to do terrible acts. Countries go to war and bar fights break out all because some guy felt disrespected. Most men who have anger issues will admit their anger is triggered when they feel dishonored.

Your husband longs to be respected by you. There is a good chance he married you because he found satisfaction in the way you showed him honor. So my question to you is this: How are you doing now?

When we were newlyweds, Rhonda did not always recognize how important her respect was to me. When she talked to me as if she were my mother, I would inadvertently discount whatever she was saying. I didn't mean to disregard her; I think it was just a subconscious defense mechanism. Have you observed your husband shutting you down when you try to "help" him accomplish a task? He may be feeling disrespected.

I remember when Rhonda had her "aha moment" and realized how her constant "reminding" me of my responsibilities was making me feel disrespected. Are your attempts to "help" your husband do better coming across as disrespectful? Sometimes letting your husband forget to follow through on a commitment is the wiser choice. Men learn from their mistakes, so letting your husband pay a late fee, run out of gas, or miss an appointment may do more to help him remember next time than your reminders.

When you ask your husband to take care of something for you, you would do well to realize men don't mean to put it out of their minds—men compartmentalize. So when we direct our full attention to one task, we may forget or delay doing something else our wives have asked us to do.

Don't interpret your husband's forgetfulness as him not caring enough about you to do what you have asked. Sometimes a husband will want to do a task his own way, but because he knows his wife will badger him until he does it her way, he will avoid the job altogether.

And then sometimes we men just forget! Most men, when they realize they've let their wives down, become disappointed in themselves and even berate themselves in their thoughts. If you chastise your husband while he is processing his own disappointment in himself, don't be surprised if your husband responds with anger—or as I did with Rhonda, shuts you down.

You have to *think* honorably toward your husband
in order to show him genuine respect.

As Rhonda learned to let me off the hook when I didn't come through for her, I found myself trying harder. And because Rhonda worked to think honorable thoughts toward me—even when I didn't do things the way she wanted me to—she would respond to me in a respectful manner. This made me gravitate toward her even more. (In case you are wondering, your husband knows when you are disappointed in him, even if you don't say a word. You have to *think* honorably toward your husband in order to show him genuine respect.)

When you learn to give your husband the respect he so desperately needs from you, you'll be blessing him with an incredible gift. Husbands hear their married friends complain all the time about how their wives dishonor them. What if your husband was one of the few who could say, "Not my wife—she is my greatest supporter"? Can you imagine how the ability to say this would stir your husband's feelings of love toward you?

And when you honor your husband, you will also be walking in obedience to the Lord's command: "Let the wife see that she respects her husband" (Ephesians 5:33 esv). During many years of biblical counseling with couples, I have seen marriages transformed when the wife learns to unconditionally respect her husband. God gave your husband a longing for respect, and it is the Lord who will bless you—and your marriage—when you learn to satisfy this desire. And don't be surprised if your respect kindles in your husband a deeper love for you and a bond of unity that will stand the tests of time.

Wives, listen to chapter 2 audio "How He Defines Respect"
at **RhondaStoppe.com/marriage-mentor**

Man to Man

When I first took the job as senior pastor, I remember Rhonda attempting to "help" me do my job by regularly telling me what the women in the church wanted me to do to help their husbands. Every time Rhonda would say, "You *need* to call this man because his wife said such-and-such," the hair on the back of my neck would bristle and I found myself pulling away from her.

While I knew Rhonda was sincerely trying to help, her attempts made me feel like she didn't think I was up to the task of pastoring, so she somehow needed to persuade me to step up my game. I was relieved when Rhonda realized how disrespected she was making me feel.

In this chapter Rhonda shared with your wife how feeling respected is likely your number one need as a husband—as a man, really. Have you ever experienced a time when you felt like you were "all that and a bag of chips"? Maybe everything at work was going well; you landed that deal, built that wall, or achieved something you've been working hard to accomplish. You came home at the end of a workday all ready to bless your household, and you were met by a wife who was exasperated from a hard day at work or at home with the kids. She didn't even give you a chance to talk before she ticked off a list of how you've not measured up to her expectations.

Wow. In one moment everything changed, right? The rug

was pulled out and you were deflated. How do you handle such times? Are you tempted to think thoughts like, *She doesn't give me the respect I deserve. I'm doing the best I can, and she won't even acknowledge how hard I work?*

When your mind starts down this path, be aware that pride is crouching at the door. Elevating yourself will put you in a dangerous situation both in your marriage and in life. We men are often motivated by our pride, are we not? The world tells us it's just part of being a man, so when we are not given the respect we think we deserve, we can feel justified in how we respond.

When you are not appreciated, do you impulsively react from a place of arrogance and pride? What's your knee-jerk response when you feel dishonored? Do you withdraw? Or maybe you lash out in anger, harsh demands, or some other behavior that promotes your own agenda.

While these responses seem natural, for a godly man they are not. If you are a Christian, God has promised to give you a new life in Christ that reflects the humble character of His Son. If you are truly a believer, your sin of pride should make you miserable—no matter how much you try to justify it.

James 4:6 tells us that God is so against pride He resists a proud person. Thinking about how to respond in humility is counter to our culture and our natural minds. But if you choose humility over pride in how you respond to disrespect, what a great model of grace and mercy that will be for your family and others to observe.

I'm not talking about being a weak man who rolls over when confronted. Rather, I am talking about a man who is strong. Stronger than your urge to lash out. Strong enough to choose to humble yourself under the mighty hand of God, who will exalt you in due time (see 1 Peter 5:6).

God promises that He will give grace to the humble. I don't know about you, but to me, holding on to my pride isn't worth losing out on God's grace. Don't you agree?

So, what can you do if your wife refuses to realize her disrespect toward you is more than just hurtful to you? How can you help her see it is really rebellion toward God? I suggest you do what God tells you to do in Colossians 3:19: "Husbands, love your wives…" Oh, wait. There's more. Here are other principles you'll find in that passage:

- Do not treat your wife harshly.
- Love her in a way that pleases the Lord.
- Love her without condition (the same way you want to be respected without condition).
- Serve your wife the way you vowed to on the day you said, "I do."

First Peter 3:7 (ASV) tells husbands to live with wives "according to knowledge." This means to dwell with them in an understanding way. How, you might ask? You've got to go to school and learn what makes your wife tick. And then Peter adds an interesting statement: "That your prayers may not be hindered."

What? Can you imagine taking the time to pray, only to realize your prayers have just bounced off the ceiling because of your disobedience to our Savior's Word concerning your wife? There you are, pouring your heart out to God, telling Him how badly your wife is treating you, and God is figuratively putting His hands over His ears, saying, "La, la, la, la, la, I can't hear you." All because of this one thing you decided to ignore: living with your wife in an understanding way.

Wow, that is some sobering stuff! Can it really mean that God will ignore your prayers? Are you going to take a chance that God won't listen to your prayers for your wife to change, for your children to follow Christ, or for your life to honor the Lord? I'm not willing to question if God means what He says. How about you?

Practical Advice

So let's say you're working to show love toward your wife, but her habit of disrespecting you does not seem to change. What can you do?

First off, choose to believe that your wife does love you and wants to work toward a better marriage. First Corinthians 13:7 says love "believes all things." This means choosing to believe the best about your wife is an act of love. The fact that she is reading this book reveals her desire to work on being a better wife to you and improving your life together. I'm thinking that's a good thing.

So, believing she does love you, realize how you can help her respond in a way that speaks love to you. The next time your wife reacts in a disrespectful manner, rather than recoil or lash out, ask God to help you teach her how her words belittle you as a man.

Then wait for an opportunity to talk to your wife when neither of you are tired or hungry so your words will be well received. Choose a time when you are alone—away from people and not in front of the children. Remember, your goal is not to shame, manipulate, or embarrass your wife, but rather to help her understand how her words make you feel disrespected. As you calmly and lovingly make yourself vulnerable to your wife, she might truly consider your words. And that is where real change begins.

From a Wife's Perspective
A Word from Rhonda

For many years I did not understand how my husband's need to be respected by me meant as much to him as my desire to feel loved by him did to me. Your wife may not know this about you either. In the above chapter, I shared with her insights into how she can show you respect—and things that may make you feel dishonored to change. So pray for God to guide her to make these changes.

Do you realize that more than anything, your wife wants

to think you have warm, fuzzy feelings toward her? She likely knows you respect the work she does to keep your lives running smoothly, but in my experience as a marriage mentor, most wives fear their husband's love for them does not run as deeply as they had hoped. And that makes them feel insecure and unlovely.

Taking time to love your wife with your words and kind gestures may make all the difference in helping her respond to you with the honor you crave.

If you want your wife to treat you with respect, make it easy for her to do so by treating her in a way that speaks love to her. Taking time to love your wife with your words and kind gestures may make all the difference in helping her respond to you with the honor you crave.[5]

Together, watch chapter 2 video at
RhondaStoppe.com/marriage-mentor

Thinking It Through

Has God convicted you of any areas in which you are withholding respect for your husband or love for your wife? Take some time to ask the Lord to forgive you and help you turn from your sin.

Living It Out

Wives: In a discussion with your husband, finish this sentence: "I want you to know how much I respect you. Here are things I respect about you that I often recognize but rarely put into words:

_____."

Husbands: Consider the qualities you love about your wife. Recall the things that made you fall in love with her in the first place. In a conversation with your wife, finish this sentence: "Some of the things I love about you that often cross my mind but are hard for me to put into words are:

_____."

If answering these questions aloud is difficult for you, consider writing a letter, an e-mail, or even a text. The point is to put into words what your spouse longs to hear. So do this in whatever way you're most comfortable.

One of the best ways to learn to interact with your spouse in the way they desire is to fellowship with couples who have learned the secret of unconditional love and respect. Look for married couples in your church whom you would like to emulate and spend time with them.

3

We're falling Out of Love

WHAT TO DO WHEN LOVE STARTS TO FADE

"Is this really my life?" the young bride said through tears. Theresa couldn't believe she found herself "falling out of love" with the man she had vowed to love forever only 18 months earlier.

Theresa composed herself and told me the story of the whirlwind romance that led up to her marriage. As she shared with me how she and her husband met, I saw a sparkle in her eye and a gentle smile across her lips. When she talked about the long walks she and her fiancé would take on the beach, holding hands and dreaming about how happy they would be as husband and wife, another tear trickled down her cheek.

What had happened? Theresa couldn't point to any particular event that had caused her feelings for her husband to change. It had all happened gradually. "Life just got in the way" was how she put it.

What's the Key to Staying in Love?

Theresa's story is not uncommon. Many couples find themselves in trouble when they wrongly make the tasks of everyday living their priority rather than nurturing their love for one another. So how can you cultivate a loving relationship with your husband that will stand the test of time?

The first insight into building a love that lasts is to take your focus off of how much you want to be loved by your husband. If you become obsessed with your longing to feel loved, you will become more preoccupied with self-satisfaction than with building a happy relationship. And this, in turn, will undermine the health of your marriage.

You may be surprised to learn the secret to loving your husband well lies in learning to love God deeply. Because when your love for the Lord is genuine, He gives you His supernatural ability to love others selflessly—including your husband.

The marriages I most want to emulate are those of husbands and wives who have learned to love God so much that their passion for one another is almost supernatural. Don't you want a marriage like that?

So how can you learn to love God so deeply that it spills over into your marriage? Jesus said the greatest priority of life is to "love the LORD your God with all your heart, with all your soul, with all your mind, and with all your strength" (Mark 12:30).

Let's take a closer look at Jesus' words, shall we? Notice how He said you are to love God: with *all* your heart, *all* your soul, *all* your mind, *all* your strength. It's an all-out love. It holds nothing back. And it involves every part of your being—your emotions, your inner self, and your thoughts. This kind of love seeks to grow closer to God and know Him intimately. That's how you fall more and more in love with someone—by getting to know them.

When Love Starts to Fade

Along with growing your love for the Lord, here are three practical steps you can take when you notice that your love for your husband is fading:

Repent

Even though Steve and I have biblically counseled married couples for many years, it still surprises me when spouses are convinced that the trouble in their marriage is no fault of their own. When a wife has this outlook, she has usually become so focused on how her husband has not measured up to her expectations that she is unable to see her own contribution to the discord.

Might that describe you? Asking God to help search your heart and make you aware of your sin is the first step toward repentance. To repent requires you to agree with God that your thoughts and attitudes are sinful. It is easy to make excuses or justify sinful acts, so take some time to be alone with the Lord and pray, "Search me, O God, and know my heart; try me, and know my anxieties; and see if there is any wicked way in me, and lead me in the way everlasting" (Psalm 139:23-24).

If the Holy Spirit reveals to you areas of dissatisfaction toward your husband, will you agree with God that your resentment is sin? And will you confess your sin?

I know, I know—I can hear you saying, "But you don't know my husband. Why doesn't *he* have to repent?" You're right—I don't know your husband, but God does. And only God can do a work in your husband, not you. If God reveals to you areas of sin that you are harboring against your husband, ask Him to make you truly contrite over your sin. Then commit to daily asking God to make your heart tender toward your husband. To soften your heart is not beyond His power.

The next step to rekindling your love for your husband is…

Remember

Take a moment to think back to the way things were when you fell in love with your husband. You thought about him throughout the day. You looked him in the eye when he talked, and you listened intently to what he had to say. Remember how you would tell your girlfriends the qualities you loved about him?

One of my favorite dating memories took place when I was 15 years old. Steve and I were just starting to become interested in one another. One night I arrived at our school's gymnasium, where I would be cheerleading for our basketball team. When I walked into the gym, Steve had just dribbled a basketball down the court. As he came down from shooting a layup, we were face-to-face. It was a moment frozen in time. Our eyes met, he smiled, and then he ran back down the court to join his team. That magical moment is forever burned in my memory as the instant I fell in love with my husband.

Do you remember a time when you couldn't wait for your husband's gaze to meet yours? A moment in particular that took your breath away? When you make a habit of remembering details of how you and your husband fell in love, you can rekindle feelings of adoration you may have forgotten. Looking at old pictures, reading old love notes, and just talking about past memories with your husband can have a wonderfully positive influence on your relationship.

Believe the Best About Your Husband

Relationships in which people always believe the best about you are priceless, wouldn't you agree? Would your husband count you as one of those relationships? Does he have the confidence you will cover his mistakes with kindness? Or does he worry, *I wonder how I will disappoint her today?*

When you think about your husband, do you tend to dwell on the things about him that disappoint you? Left unchecked, this practice can seriously undermine your love for your husband. The result will be dissatisfaction with your marriage. And over time you may find yourself coming to believe, *I am falling out of love with my husband.*

So what can you do? How can you cultivate a new way of thinking about your husband?

It starts by making a deliberate decision to think on his good qualities and refuse to dwell on how he doesn't make you happy. In this way you can rekindle your affection for your husband and learn to delight in him. And what husband doesn't want to be enjoyed by his wife?

What a gift you give your man when you determine to take pleasure in his good qualities and overlook his less-than-admirable ones. Wouldn't you want your husband to do this for you as well? Let this behavior begin with you.

Whenever your husband does something that displeases you, determine that you will continue to think the best of him. Don't be quick to assign wrong motives to his actions. For example, when you go to the bathroom in the middle of the night and fall into the toilet because he left the seat up, don't angrily assume he doesn't care enough about you to put down the seat. No, simply realize that he forgot. And then choose to forgive him for his forgetfulness. Wouldn't you want your husband to forgive you when you inadvertently forget to do something he has asked you to do? Offer him the same grace you hope he will extend to you.

The Power of Right Thoughts

A great way to develop a healthy thought life toward your husband is to follow the advice of the apostle Paul: "Whatever is true, whatever is honorable, whatever is just, whatever is pure, whatever is lovely, whatever is commendable, if there is any excellence, if there is anything worthy of praise, think about these things" (Philippians 4:8 ESV).

At this point you may be thinking, *What difference will it make if I try to think on what is best about my husband? He will never be anything but negative and unappreciative.*

I know a woman who would beg to differ. Her name is Anne.

Anne had been married for more than a decade to a man she had learned to "tolerate," as she put it. But after her pastor gave a sermon on Philippians 4:8, she determined she would make every effort to have only good and honorable thoughts about her husband, Ted.

At first Anne could hardly find any good thoughts to replace the negative ones. But with God's help and a resolve to heal her marriage, Anne disciplined herself to put out of her mind any negative thoughts she had. Instead, she tried to dwell on positive thoughts about Ted.

As Anne's thought life was being transformed, her attitudes and actions were also changing. Soon Anne was not only thinking well of her husband; she also made it a point to verbally affirm him.

After experiencing so many years of Anne's sharp tongue and condescending tone, Ted was wary of her new demeanor. He had learned a long time ago to keep his mouth shut, watch TV until bedtime, and not cross his wife if he wanted a relaxing evening. Over time Ted grew to trust that Anne's new manner was not a passing phase. He found himself looking forward to arriving home after work. He even started to linger in the kitchen after dinner to talk with Anne as she cleaned up the dinner dishes.

One day Ted told Anne, "I'll do the dishes tonight, honey. You do so much for me and the kids. It's the least I can do." Anne just about fell out of her chair.

It has been more than ten years since Anne determined to think what was best about Ted. She will tell you that decision saved her marriage. And because of Anne's example, Ted has learned to do the same and dwell on her good qualities as well. Today their marriage is one that others desire to emulate.

But My Husband Doesn't Deserve It

You may be tempted to say, "You don't know how my husband has disappointed me. He doesn't deserve for me to focus on his good qualities because they could never outweigh his bad ones."

God could make the same statement about you—and me. Our feeble human attempts to do good will never outweigh our bad. The prophet Isaiah said, "All our righteousnesses are like filthy rags" (Isaiah 64:6). The original Hebrew text in this passage reveals that by "filthy rags," Isaiah meant menstrual rags. Yuck! I think the prophet wanted to impress on us how little God values our religious practices apart from loving Him. This gives a real picture of how impossible it is for our good deeds to ever make up for our bad.

Are You Merciful?

God's love is merciful. His mercy not only forgives our sins but covers our weaknesses and provides relief from penalty.

Do you look for ways to come alongside your husband's weaknesses to be his helper, or do you watch for him to make mistakes so you can point them out, belittle him in front of the kids, or publicly ridicule him? Such actions are not merciful.

In case you may think showing mercy is optional, Jesus commanded His followers, "Be merciful, just as your Father also is merciful."[1] Are you ready to ask God to help you be merciful toward your husband no matter what? In so doing, your attitude toward him is sure to reflect God's grace. And as you make it a habit to cover your husband's shortcomings with compassion, you might find him responding in kind.

The final step for relighting your love for your husband is…

Return

Back when you and your husband were dating, what were some of the things you did to win his heart? How might you return to carrying out those actions?

When Steve and I were dating, he drove a really cool car—a Ford Mustang Mach 1. The car's muffler could be heard rumbling down the street from a block away. I remember choosing just the right outfit, putting on my makeup, and curling my hair in anticipation of our date. Inevitably I would hear the deep rumbling of Steve's car as I was spraying the final mist of hairspray on my hair and checking my makeup one last time. My heart would skip a beat knowing that my love would soon arrive to pick me up for our date.

When your husband is about to arrive home from work, do you anticipate his return? Do you put in the same effort to look nice as you did when you were dating? It's easy for wives to make sure they are looking their best whenever they go out in public yet become lazy about their appearance at home.

In her book *For Women Only*, Shaunti Feldhahn invited men to anonymously express some of their deepest desires for their marriage relationship. Listen to what one man said about what it means to him when his wife doesn't keep up her appearance: "When you don't take care of yourself, I feel unvalued and unhappy."[2]

Men have this secret affirmation they give one another when they see a man whose wife makes an effort to look pretty. I have heard men say, "It's really not about if she is the perfect size." Rather, they are affirmed when, through her appearance, the woman on their arm says to the world, "I care about this man. I value him. I dress for him. I am his prize." Do you carry yourself as if you are your husband's prize?

I remember the day I realized I had been letting myself go. Somewhere amidst my kids' toddler years, I looked in the mirror after my husband had arrived home from work and saw how bad I looked! I walked out of our bedroom and asked him, "How long have I looked this bad?" He just smiled and said, "You're busy with the kids all day," then winked at me. The poor guy. Notice he did not say, "Oh, honey, you don't look bad." From that day on I determined to prepare myself each day to look pretty for Steve's homecoming.

What are some other ways you caught your husband's affections in the past that you could return to today? Here are some actions you might want to try:

- When he talks to you, stop what you are doing and look at him.
- Laugh out loud at his jokes—even if you are so familiar with them the punch lines no longer take you by surprise.
- Don't talk to him like you are his mother. (We will talk more about this later.)
- Tell him what you admire about him—often.
- Thank him for working to help support the family. (And if he is out of work, find other accomplishments to praise—even if it is something as simple as remembering to put down the toilet seat!)
- Be his girlfriend. This means sit with him while he works on a project, go to the hardware store with him, go out with him to his favorite burger joint.
- Find reasons to touch him. Scratch his back. Rub his neck. Hold his hand.
- Have sex with him. (We will talk more about this in chapter 7.)

This list is certainly not exhaustive, but hopefully it will help get you started on thinking about the many ways you can fan the flames of love for your husband. And when you are trying to rekindle your love for him, remember you are not alone. God wants you to learn to love your husband with His merciful love. He will gladly help you. All you need to do is ask (see James 4:2).

Did you know God is more interested in you having a loving marriage than you are? He is the One who can heal your marriage and make your love last a lifetime.

When you begin with an authentic love for the Lord, God's love will spill out of your heart and into your marriage.

When you begin with an authentic love for the Lord, God's love will spill out of your heart and into your marriage. When this happens, your marriage will become the most glorious of all your earthly relationships. And when you tap into this delightful resource, you will discover the secret to growing more in love with your husband with each passing year. In time, the love displayed in your marriage will be the kind others will want to emulate.

From a Husband's Perspective
A Word from Steve

This chapter talks about some expectations you may have for a loving marriage. You want your husband to be everything you imagined he would be, but let's face it—we as men fall short. It hurts me to write this statement as much as it does for you to hear it.

Like your husband, there are times when I am anything but attentive. However, Rhonda covers this with love—Christ's love. Was this always the case? No. Over the years, she has learned to love Christ first, and her love for me spills out from her passion for Christ.

I challenge you to apply the principles Rhonda laid out in this chapter and see if God can use your love and obedience for Him to influence a more loving response from your husband. If you don't see a positive result right away, don't give up. When you commit to living in obedience to God's plan for a loving marriage, He will bless you for your faithfulness.

Even if your husband doesn't respond initially the way you would like, your commitment to loving God with your whole heart will be rewarded. The godly life you lead may eventually stir in your husband a desire to obey the Lord as well. And consider how your children will learn to love when they observe your unconditional love for their father—no matter how he responds. By simply adjusting your mind to think well of your husband, you are laying up treasure in heaven. An eternal reward for temporal obedience sounds like a great layaway plan, don't you agree?

In the many years that I have biblically counseled married couples, I have seen marriages transformed when wives committed to thinking well of their husbands. If your husband is able to rest in knowing you think well of him, you will become his delight.

When you become a joy to your husband, his love for you is sure to grow. And when you are thinking only what is good about your husband, your heart will be filled with love for him as well.

Wives, listen to chapter 3 audio "Staying in Love" at
RhondaStoppe.com/marriage-mentor

Man to Man

Staying in love—it really is all in your mind.

Well...you got her! Remember all the time you spent pursuing your wife, trying to get her attention? And how happy you were when she returned your affections?

I remember when I was dating Rhonda. She was the belle of the ball, a real looker, who in my opinion was the one everyone was trying to date. But no one else could have her because she was mine—due to my suave personality and heavenly good looks (I may have stretched that description just a bit, but it's my story, so I'll tell it how I like to remember it).

I was so glad I was the one who got to date Rhonda and one day to make her my bride. It's funny how after being married a while those feelings of accomplishment and satisfaction were overshadowed when I started realizing this girl had some traits that were a bit less than desirous. For one thing she would literally freak out if I left crumbs on the counter in the kitchen after she cleaned—who does that?

It wasn't long before I found myself focusing on those things I felt were trouble areas and completely overlooked the fact that this girl was the one I wanted, the one I won at the envy of all my friends (or at least in my mind I thought they were envious—again, this is my story!).

Soon it occurred to me that what I was choosing to focus on about Rhonda's shortcomings had started to undermine how I felt toward my wife. Maybe you've been there too. It's easy to focus on the negative—those characteristics that you likely overlooked early in your relationship.

If your mind tends to dwell on your disappointments, what really happened is at some point you stopped looking at all the things that drew you to your wife and started thinking on the things about her that bother you. You likely feel a sense of betrayal because she has ceased to meet up to your expectations. But beware, if you keep going down this path of wrong thinking, just as your mind instructed your heart to love your wife while you were dating, your negative thoughts can draw your heart away from her until you start to believe you're falling out of love with your wife.

Just a note: Aren't you glad the Creator of this universe doesn't do that to you? I'm sure if you're honest you could come up with a list of how you have not lived up to the expectations God would have for your life. And yet He continues to love you without condition. Remember, the Bible instructs husbands to love their wives as Christ loves the church. How does the way you love your wife measure up to that standard?

Ask God to help you develop the habit
of thinking lovingly toward your wife.

What to Do

If after honest evaluation you realize you have been thinking wrongly toward your wife, there are steps you can take to get back on track:

1. Confess to God any bitterness, unforgiveness, anger, or other areas of resentment that you may be embracing against your wife.

2. Consider changing the focus of your thoughts. Thinking right thoughts toward your wife is the first step toward staying in love and having God's peace in your marriage, so ask God to help you develop the habit of thinking lovingly toward your wife.

3. Put away childish behaviors and desires. Did I just tell you to grow up? Well, yes—yes, I did. If you are being driven by your wants, desires, and expectations, then it's time to evaluate your maturity as a believer.

4. Remember the qualities that drew you to your wife in the first place. It's interesting how many times God tells us to go back and remind ourselves of what we have learned. Listen to the words of the apostle Peter, who understood the value of a good reminder: "(I stir up your pure minds by way of reminder), that you may be mindful of the words which were spoken" (2 Peter 3:1-2).

From a Wife's Perspective
A Word from Rhonda

Staying in love really is all in your mind. I realize over the years I've often not measured up to Steve's expectations, but knowing that he is committed not to dwell on my shortcomings makes me feel loved and secure, and causes me to love and trust him all the more.

When I think of marriages I want to emulate, there are two people who come to mind who have learned the secret of disciplining their minds to think whatever is good about their spouse. Don't you want to be that kind of couple?

In the above chapter, I talked to your wife about right thinking. If this is an area where she has been struggling, it is my prayer that she will implement the biblical principles I laid out to help her achieve victory over negative thoughts.

Let it begin with you.

Whether or not you see your wife working toward change, let it begin with you. God promises peace to anyone who thinks in the way laid out in Philippians 4:8. So adjusting your thought life from negative to positive will set your mind free from the unrest caused by habitual wrong thinking. When you become a husband whom your wife trusts to think the best about her, she will feel secure and loved and hopefully will respond to you with honoring thoughts as well.

Together, watch chapter 3 video at
RhondaStoppe.com/marriage-mentor

Thinking It Through

1. You fell in love with each other because your mind instructed your heart how to feel. Take some time to consider and then share with one another one or two characteristics about your spouse that caused you to fall in love with them.

2. Write out Philippians 4:8. Using this scripture as a guide,

name two positive thoughts about your spouse you will
commit to dwelling on this week.

Living It Out

Create Magical Moments

A key part of becoming a couple who stays in love is commit-
ting yourselves to creating memorable encounters that celebrate your love. How can you create these magical moments?
You don't have to plan an expensive date. On the contrary, frequently the most romantic interactions between couples are
simple and occur in the course of everyday life.

Here are a few ways to put some magic back into your marriage:

Never underestimate the power of a wink and a smile.

---

1. Make eye contact from across a crowded room, and give
   a flirtatious smile or a wink. For example, the other day
   Steve came with me to a radio interview. During the radio
   program, he was in the sound booth with the technicians.
   When I glanced at him during the interview, he gave
   me a quick wink and it took my breath away. With that
   simple gesture, my heart melted and I had to work to stay
   focused on the point I was making to the radio host. Never
   underestimate the power of a wink and a smile.

2. Send a loving or flirtatious text in the middle of the day.
   (Be careful what you say in your text in case one day your

14-year-old picks up your phone and sees your flirtatious comments—we speak from experience!)

3. Be creative. Try to recall what you did to capture your love's attention when you were dating. And then work to rekindle the magic like you did back then.

4

Your Marriage Can Survive Toddlers and Teens

MARRIAGE SURVIVAL GUIDE FOR PARENTS

After Steve and I had been married a couple of years, I began to get the baby bug. My girlfriend Beth had recently given birth to an adorable baby girl. Whenever Beth and her husband, Dave, would come over to our house, I would watch longingly as Beth nurtured her baby, Kristal.

Kristal was one of those babies who loved the baby swing. She would sit for hours in the swing with her pacifier in her mouth as Beth, Dave, Steve, and I would visit and play games late into the evenings. The joy I observed in our friends was so precious I was certain having a baby was "just what our marriage needed."

When I approached Steve about this, his practical response was, "What—now? We just bought this house. We are living in the mess of this huge remodel and you want a *baby*?"

I knew Steve was right to question the rationale of wanting a baby at that time in our lives. We had agreed to move into the house we had purchased so we could use all our money to remodel it rather than renting an apartment while the work was being done. And to top it off, my income was what we used to make the house payment while

Steve's income paid for all other bills and the materials needed for the remodel. Since Steve and I had already promised each other I would quit my job to be a stay-at-home mom once we had kids, I can see now how the thought of having children would have weighed heavily on Steve's already strained budget plans.

However, at the time, all I could see was how badly I wanted to be a mother. And each time we enjoyed time with Beth and Dave, I was even more convinced our marital bliss would not be complete until we could procreate!

As the months passed and Steve watched Kristal become more than just a squirming little newborn, I saw a new interest spark in him. Steve loved playing with Kristal and was overjoyed when he could get her to laugh out loud at his silliness.

When Steve and I finally had a serious talk about having a baby, I assured him I most likely wouldn't get pregnant right away. Some of my girlfriends had taken up to a year to conceive. With a deep breath, and a prayer gently whispered, Steve agreed to "try" to have a baby.

About a month later, Beth and Dave came to our house again for a visit. We ate our usual snacks—including my husband's favorite potato chips and onion dip. The next day while I was at work, I kept burping that nasty onion dip. And two days later, I was still burping. That's when I thought, *I wonder if this is morning sickness.*

During my lunch hour I visited my doctor. After I returned to work, the doctor's office called with the message, "Mrs. Stoppe, your test is positive." I wasn't sure exactly what that meant, so I asked, "Positive what? Positive I'm pregnant, or positive I'm not?" (At the time I was thinking, *Steve will think it's a positive thing if my test turns out negative.*)

As it turned out, I *was* pregnant. Our first child, Meredith, was born on Christmas Eve. I was so happy to bring our little bundle of joy home and start living as a family that I left the hospital the very next day—and besides, it was Christmas.

As time passed and we settled into our routines, Steve and I made an alarming discovery. Our baby, Meredith, was nothing like Kristal. Whereas Kristal would gladly accept a pacifier, Meredith would gag and spit it out. Kristal would sit in the baby swing for hours on end, but Meredith would freak out and cry because the swing terrified her. And while Kristal would sleep soundly in her bed each evening, Meredith screamed wildly for hours on end. (Since I didn't know much about babies, it wasn't until Beth's mother came over for a visit that she informed me the reason Meredith pulled up her knees and screamed each night was because she had colic.)

This turned out to be the hardest year of our marriage. Up to this point, we had agreed on pretty much everything we did as a couple. But now disagreements were more frequent. For example, because of Meredith's constant crying, I became frazzled, exhausted, and an emotional wreck. When I would ask Steve to take Meredith for a walk so she would feel better, he insisted she needed to "cry it out" in her crib. Since we didn't see eye to eye on how to deal with Meredith's crying, I worried, *How many other things will we disagree on as we raise this child?*

The irony of all this is I had originally anticipated only the bliss that having a baby would bring. I hadn't expected the difficulties and exhaustion as well. Maybe you can relate?

After three long months of constant crying, Meredith woke up one morning as a happy baby. No more tummy trouble, and from that day on, she has been an absolute delight. (Meredith—if you're reading this, please know how very thankful we are for you, and in hindsight, we even thank the Lord for the work He did in us as you cried your little eyes out.)

Iron Sharpens Iron

Raising children is sure to invite friction into a marriage. Not only are parents passionate about their kids, they are emotionally vested as well—even to the point of being unreasonable sometimes. Let me explain: in nearly 20 years of youth ministry work, Steve and I encountered many parents who were blinded by their passion for their kids. For example, moms will go to great lengths to defend their child if they feel a teacher is treating him or her unjustly—even when it's clear the child is the one at fault.

Most parents have strong opinions about how their kids should be disciplined, what they should be allowed to do, and so on. But when

Mom and Dad disagree on these important issues, sparks will fly. If you and your husband disagree about a specific parenting issue and the friction causes the two of you to evaluate your motives and surrender to Christ's leading, then you will become sharpened instruments for the Master's use.

However, when conflict over your kids leads you to sinful actions, you can know your motivations are not in line with God's will. In the middle of parenting disagreements when you react sinfully to your husband, do you stop to evaluate why you are willing to sin in the situation? If not, you are sadly missing an opportunity God is providing for you—and your husband—to ask the Holy Spirit for help. Once you are willing to admit your own sinful motivations and bring your thoughts and actions in line with what the Bible teaches regarding your situation, you will be able to have a rational, respectful discussion with your husband.

But Girls Just Wanna Have Fun!

When Meredith was about 13, Steve was the youth pastor at a church in Austin, Texas. Steve's rule had always been that our kids were not allowed to ride in a car with a driver who was under the age of 18. But as the daughter of the youth pastor, Meredith was friends with a lot of kids under the age of 18 who had driver's licenses. Whenever she would ask if she could ride with one of her teenage friends, Steve promptly told her, "Are they 18 or older? If not, then the answer is no."

Poor Meredith. I felt so sorry for her. Since I tried very hard never to disagree with Steve's mandate in front of Meredith, she would have thought I was in complete agreement with her father's rule. But behind closed doors, Steve and I had many discussions about how unfair I thought he was being to Meredith. On one occasion I even remember crying as I told Steve he was "responding out of an irrational fear of what might happen to Meredith."

You know how you know when you've pushed your husband too far? Well, with that comment, I knew I'd done just that! Steve's nostrils flared (if you knew anything about Steve, you would know this means he is really mad), and he responded, "Fine. You let her do whatever you think is best—if you are willing to live with the consequence if something happens to her."

Seriously—how was I supposed to respond to that statement? Truth be told, over the years that Steve had been a youth pastor, we had seen our fair share of inexperienced teenage drivers get into car accidents—some of them fatal. I was more than aware of the statistics regarding teenage-driver accidents. I just wanted to believe nothing would happen to *our* daughter because these were *good kids*.

After I spent some time pondering the matter, the Holy Spirit convicted me over the fact I hadn't been honoring my husband's wishes. In the end, I stood by Steve's decision not to allow Meredith to ride with inexperienced drivers. Meredith continued to be upset, embarrassed, and distant with us whenever the issue came up.

One night after we had been out as a family, we arrived home to find a car parked in front of our house. A father of one of our youth group teens walked up to Steve's car window and tearfully explained how one of the teenage girls in the youth group, who had been driving with another friend in her car, had just been killed in an accident. I'll spare you the details, but suffice it to say, these were two good girls. There was no drinking involved, and they were not doing anything illegal. The accident was simply a result of the girl's inexperience as a driver.

We were all devastated. After the funeral, Meredith came to us to apologize for being angry about our "stupid rule" because now she understood we were just trying to protect her.

That experience made me realize how very much I needed my husband's wisdom and input when it came to decisions regarding our kids' well-being. I usually leaned toward letting the kids do what I thought would be "fun," while Steve was less concerned about their having a good time and more interested in keeping them safe and molding their character to be Christlike.

What if I had fought with Steve in front of Meredith? What if I pushed to get Steve to change his mind and Meredith had been allowed to ride with her friends? Maybe nothing bad would have happened to her. However, any bad that would have occurred would have been the consequence of my insistence, which, in turn, could have damaged our marriage—and ultimately, our family.

When you and your husband do not work to present a united front to your children, they will inevitably look for the point of your contention and get the two of you bickering over who is right so they can go on their merry way and do whatever they please.

Take a moment and evaluate the way you and your husband parent. Do you teach your kids to respect their father by how you treat him in their presence? Do you talk about your kids' father behind his back or complain to your children when your husband does not measure up to your expectations? If you do not instill a healthy respect in your kids for their father, you will suffer the consequences when you need your husband's reinforcement during their preteen and teenage years.

But What If My Husband Isn't the Best Father?

Is your husband aloof about parenting? Or possibly too controlling? I know people who fall into each of these categories. So what can you do when your husband does not measure up to your expectations as a father? For insight, let's learn from a mom whose husband was extremely controlling.

Tina's husband, Bob, had always been a control freak. When they were dating, Tina found security in Bob's take-charge manner as he planned every detail of their dates to a tee. After they were married, however, Bob's strong tendencies to control were often a point of contention. To avoid Bob's barrage of questioning when he arrived home, Tina had learned to keep certain details of how she spent her days from her husband. As time went on, Tina learned Bob's desire to control was deeply seated in fear—a fear of not being able to protect his family.

When Bob and Tina's teenage son began to resist his father's strong hand of control, intense arguments between father and son broke loose in their home. Tina felt sorry for her son and would often get into the middle of the arguments—until one day Tina's son pulled her aside and asked her to please stay out of the fight. He explained to his mother that her stepping in actually made Bob angrier and less reasonable to deal with.

As a favor to her son, Tina stepped back—way back—whenever the two would go toe to toe. That is when Tina learned to pray like she had never prayed before. While her husband and son were having heated arguments, Tina would go to her prayer chair and intercede for both of them. First, Tina would ask the Lord to reveal any sin in her heart so that she might confess it and be cleansed so her prayers would be effective (see James 5:16). Then she prayed specifically for her husband's controlling ways not to push her son into rebellion. And finally, Tina prayed for her husband to be convicted of how his fear was driving his incessant need to control everyone—and every event—in their family.

And do you know what happened? God did a work in Tina's heart. As she made a habit of meeting with the Lord and confessing her own sin in each matter, her prayers became an effective resource in resolving the conflict between her husband and son. Years have passed since those difficult days, and Tina's commitment to pray for rather than defend her son made a lasting impression on him as a man who now serves Christ. And God changed her husband, ever so slowly. Anyone who was watching how the Lord worked to resolve Bob's control issues would say the events God used were nothing short of miraculous!

Prayer Is the Key

The value of persistent, passionate prayer is one of the shining virtues in the life of Hannah, who was the mother of Samuel. In the years before Hannah was able to bear children, she endured a troubled home life. Her husband, Elkanah, was a bigamist. Because Hannah had been unable to conceive, it is likely that in order to have children, Elkanah took a second wife—Peninnah.

Can you imagine the hurt and rivalry that Elkanah invited into his home by marrying another woman? The Bible says that Elkanah preferred Hannah over Peninnah because he loved her deeply (see 1 Samuel 1:4-5). So here you have the makings for some intense rivalry all under one roof. What was Elkanah thinking?

What a mess these three had on their hands, don't you think? In the book *Twelve Extraordinary Women,* we glean this insight: "Hannah was in constant anguish because of her own infertility. She was further tormented by Peninnah's taunts. The burden and stress made life almost unbearable."[1]

Although Hannah and Elkanah's marriage was marred by tension, the two did love one another deeply. As *Twelve Extraordinary Women* says,

> Hannah's love for her husband is the first key to understanding her profound influence as a mother. Contrary to popular opinion, the most important characteristic of a godly mother is not her relationship with her *children*. It is her love for her *husband*. The love between husband and wife is the real key to a thriving family... Furthermore, all parents need to heed this lesson: what you communicate to your children through your marital relationship will stay with them for the rest of their lives. By watching how mother and father treat one another, they will learn the most fundamental lessons of life—love, self-sacrifice, integrity, virtue, sin, sympathy, compassion, understanding and forgiveness. Whatever you teach about those things, right or wrong, is planted deep within their hearts.[2]

Each year Hannah and Elkanah traveled together to the temple to worship God. One year in particular, Hannah was so sorrowful over her situation she could not even eat. (Lucky girl—whenever I am distraught, all I want to do is eat. What about you?) Despite her difficult situation, she never became embittered. Rather, she became a woman characterized by a steadfast prayer life. First Samuel 1:12 says Hannah "continued praying before the LORD."

With a broken heart, Hannah was driven to her knees. Her trials were the very tool God used to make her a woman of intense prayer. And on this particular visit to the temple, here's what Hannah said: "O LORD of hosts, if You will indeed look on the affliction of Your maidservant and remember me, and not forget Your maidservant, but will give Your maidservant a male child, then I will give him to the LORD all the days of his life" (verse 11).

And when God answered Hannah's prayer and gave her a son, her immediate response was to pray. First Samuel 2:1-10 records her words, and the prayer is a beautiful masterpiece of thanksgiving.

So Hannah's troubles taught her to pray with intense passion, and when God answered her, she continued to remain steadfast in prayer.

Hannah's difficult marriage was also the catalyst God used to cause her to dedicate Samuel to the Lord. Do you realize Samuel is one of the few men in the Bible for whom we cannot find any record of rebellion against God? What a legacy Hannah left in her son Samuel—all because she turned to God in her trial and did not become bitter or look for a way to escape her difficult marriage.

In the same way God used conflict in Hannah's home to make her a woman of prayer, the Lord wants to mold you into a woman who prays at all times, including in difficult circumstances. And if you follow Hannah's example of keeping your heart pure before the Lord, your prayers will not be hindered. Your fervent petitions for your children will do more to prepare them for God's plan for their lives than anything you can do on your own, including rescuing them from a difficult situation they may be facing.

To Know Christ and Make Him Known

If you have a personal relationship with Christ, then you have been invited to be on a mission with God. And what is that mission? To put it simply: to know Christ and to make Him known.

In your marriage relationship, do you tend to focus on how you can have a better marriage? In parenting, is your aim to become a better parent? While these are worthwhile goals, if you make them the focus of your life, you will have missed your mission. Sadly, the Christian church today leans much more toward helping people build happy lives rather than missional lives.

For example, when you got married, was your goal to live happily ever after with your husband? Have you made it your life's goal to work hard so you can have a nice home in which to raise a family? Again, these are not necessarily bad goals. The problem lies in making these "good" goals idols in your life—idols that take priority over

God's mission for you to know Christ more intimately day by day through prayer, Bible study, and fellowship with other Christians.

Reading book after book on how to be a better wife, mother, or Christian yet neglecting to spend dedicated amounts of time with God and His Word is settling for far less than what the Lord has for you. For it is through time with Him and the Bible that you will learn the character of Christ. Your love for Him will grow only as you sit in His presence and get to know Him more intimately through the pages of Scripture.

If your mission is to know Christ and make Him known, you must devote yourself to knowing Him so well that you recognize His providential hand in your own life—and that of your family.

In his book *You and Me Forever*, Francis Chan states, "[Our kids] must see the Gospel brought to life when they observe our parenting. We strive to demonstrate a beautiful picture of Christ in hopes that they will find Him attractive and give their lives to knowing Him."[3]

When your life's purpose is to know your Savior more and more with each passing day, the natural outcome will be for you to think with a biblical worldview. When this happens, you will learn to see life's ups and downs as opportunities to make Christ known to those around you—especially to your children. And the more time you spend with Jesus, the more His character will spill out of your obedient life and thus create in others a desire to know Him too.

You Are an Ambassador for Christ

The apostle Paul often found himself in circumstances much worse than any you and I will likely ever face. And yet he never lost sight of his mission to proclaim Christ. Listen as Paul pleaded with the believers in Ephesus. He urged them to be

> praying at all times in the Spirit, with all prayer and supplication. To that end, keep alert with all perseverance, making supplication for all the saints, and also for me, that words may be given to me in opening my mouth boldly to proclaim the mystery of the gospel, for which I am an

ambassador in chains, that I may declare it boldly, as I ought to speak (Ephesians 6:18-20 ESV).

If you were in prison, would your prayer request be, "Hey, guys, I'm in chains for telling people about Christ. Could you keep praying for me to have additional opportunities to speak the gospel more boldly?" You won't likely find yourself in chains anytime soon, but sometimes a difficult marriage can make you feel like you're in prison. What if God has you right where He wants you? What if, like in Paul's life, the Lord knew you would be most effective sharing with others—including your children—the hope of salvation because of your pain?

Let me put it to you this way: if the only way God can bring your kids into the kingdom is by showing them how faith in Jesus is real through your struggle, is it worth it? My friend Tina thinks it is. She said, "If my husband's controlling bent is what drove me to my knees and my son to Christ, it was all worth it!" Wow. Isn't she right?

In Christ, God has called you to be His mouthpiece to those whom He is drawing to Himself. As you grow to know God through Bible study, memorizing scripture, and prayer, you will no doubt glorify Christ, because the natural outpouring of one who knows Jesus intimately is a love for others. This love spills over first into your marriage, then to your children, and then into all the other relationships the Lord brings your way.

Second Corinthians 5:20 makes this profound statement: "Now then, we are ambassadors for Christ, as though God were pleading through us: we implore you on Christ's behalf, be reconciled to God." How does realizing you are Christ's ambassador to reconcile others to Him influence the way you relate to your husband and your children? Maybe you should take a moment to dwell on the fact the Lord has called you to be His ambassador. Then ask God to give you the courage to set aside all other pursuits—even personal happiness—to become the woman He has ordained you to be in this generation.

I meet women all the time who say they would do anything to help their children grow up to reach their fullest potential. And yet those same women often stop short of working to build a strong marriage.

Sadly, the connection they fail to make is how the length a mom will go to love her spouse with Christ's selfless love is an incredible contribution to their children's stability and well-being. And her positive influence has the potential to impact not only her own children but their children and even their children's children.

> Your kids' security lies in the health
> of your marriage relationship.

Your kids' security lies in the health of your marriage relationship. When you live with your eyes focused on the mission God has called you to—*to know Christ and make Him known*—you will have learned the key to building a no-regrets marriage. When you determine to live in a manner that reflects a genuine love for Christ—no matter how smooth or difficult your marriage relationship may be—you will do far more to draw your kids to salvation than any words you could ever say. And isn't that your ultimate goal?

From a Husband's Perspective
A Word from Steve

Adolescence is the time when your kids are sure they know more than you. When you add to that their hormonal attitudes, dealing with them can cause strain on you and your marriage. Reading Christian parenting books and finding godly women to mentor you during this season of motherhood are great resources to guide you through this confusing time. (If you're the mother of a son, Rhonda has written a book called *Moms Raising Sons to Be Men* that is filled with biblical wisdom for moms.)

If you find yourself in the season of tweens and teens, be encouraged that somewhere around their second year of high school, most kids level off and turn back into the people you came to know and love. Truth be told, some of my finest memories with my children are from their terrible twos and trying teen years. While those times were tough to get through, they were years that forced me to have thoughtful conversations with my wife and my kids. Not to mention they kept me constantly in prayer for God to capture their hearts.

When Your Husband Won't Take the Lead

Now, you may be thinking, *Well that's fine for you that your kids' adolescent years brought you to your knees in prayer, but what about those of us whose husbands don't take that approach?*

Perhaps your husband doesn't take on the role of spiritual leader in your home. My heart goes out to you. Rhonda and I have prayed with many tearful wives who long for their husband to guide their family in spiritual matters. Maybe you would be happy if your husband would just attend church with you on Sundays. So what can you do? First realize that manipulating, crying, or pouting until your husband gives in to your demands is not the right course of action.

When my friend Ken was more interested in pursuing entertainment than guiding his family spiritually, his wife, Dorinda, quietly prayed for God to change his heart. And do you know what? After a long season of waiting for God to do His work in Ken's heart, the Lord answered Dorinda's prayer.

Learn from Dorinda's example. If you long for your husband to be a better spiritual leader so that your children will have a godly model and might be more obedient, don't nag him until he agrees to change. Nagging never works with husbands. In fact, if Rhonda nags me, I tend to want to do the opposite of what she asks.

Instead, first search your own heart and motives before the Lord. Ask God to help you not resent your husband if he is not the godly leader you had hoped he would be. Once your heart is right with God, you're ready to pray effectively and diligently each day for the Lord to transform your husband—and your children—with the truth.

Whatever stresses you may experience in your marriage (and when you are raising children together, there will be seasons of stress), remember that the answer is not to stand against one another in conflict but to stand united in prayer. Pray for your husband, and pray for your kids.

Because the Bible promises, "The prayer of a righteous person has great power as it is working."[4]

> Wives, listen to chapter 4 audio "Your Marriage, A Light to Your Kids" at **RhondaStoppe.com/marriage-mentor**

Man to Man

My friend Ken devoted his life to working hard—and playing hard. His free time was spent on all sorts of recreational activities from motorcycle riding and sailing to muscle cars. Although these hobbies were not bad in and of themselves, the time Ken spent enjoying them consumed his weekends, and on most Sundays kept him away from church. All the while Ken's wife, Dorinda, continued to take their children to church every week. And she quietly prayed for the Lord to convict her husband regarding his misguided pursuits.

Ken's preoccupation with self had taken from Dorinda a husband who was once devoted to Christ. And it pulled Ken far away from any kind of ministry for the Lord. After a number of years, the Spirit began to show Ken that he was wasting his life. One day Ken reluctantly agreed to attend a particular Bible study our church was offering to our men's group.[5]

As Ken studied how men in the Bible experienced God when they walked in obedience to Him, he came to understand that he would need to reevaluate the way he was living. After a season of wrestling with God over his newfound convictions, Ken realized the priority of his life needed to be loving God with all his heart, soul, mind, and strength (see Mark 12:30).

It was then that Ken said, "I need to adjust my life to reflect what I have been learning."

At last, Dorinda's prayers were answered! Ken was ready to make knowing Christ and making Him known the supreme priorities of his life.

As a result, Ken got rid of many of his toys and set aside some of his hobbies to become a faithful follower of Christ. Talk about a transformation! Dorinda was overjoyed as she witnessed her husband's newfound passion to serve the Lord.

Do you identify with Ken's story? Are you less than a godly leader for your family because the cares of this world—whether career or entertainment—have become a distraction? Consider how Ken's wife prayed for God to change his heart. Maybe your wife is praying for you too. Is it time to adjust your life as well?

Momma Comes First

Until kids came along, your marriage may have been pretty easy. When our first baby was born with colic, the constant crying brought unexpected stress because we were both uncertain how to handle the situation. As a man, my tendency is to try and fix or rescue my wife from whatever stresses her out, but we were both at a loss to know what to do with the incessant crying, and it *was* stressful.

When our kids were adolescents, we again found ourselves in uncharted territory that also caused stress. Because we had been in youth ministry, we had seen how marriages tend to fall apart during their kids' teenage years, so we determined to work through our season relying on each other with our eyes on Christ.

I remember one day when our adolescent son Brandon was having an attitude toward Rhonda. As adolescent boys will do, he was disrespecting and challenging his mother. When I came home to Rhonda in tears, I took Brandon aside for one of those father-son talks that likely made him wonder if he was going to live to tell about it. I said, "I will not allow you to treat my wife like this. She may be your mom, but she's *my* wife, and you'll not treat her with such disrespect."

Choosing to side with Rhonda and to support her that day—and the days following—strengthened our marriage in ways I had not expected. Regarding my stepping into their conflict, Rhonda says, "I felt like a damsel in distress who was rescued by her knight in armor."

Remember, your kids will grow up and move away. Ministering to one another while setting up boundaries for your children's behavior will grow deep your love for one another—even when kids might work to drive you apart. (As a note, if you're in a blended family situation, this is even more complicated as kids attempt to manipulate their biological parent to choose them over their marriage partner.[6])

As a dad, it is your responsibility to have your family involved in a local church where they can hear the preaching of the Word and connect with youth pastors or other godly mentors to help walk with them through the uncertain teenage years. Note that I didn't just suggest you *send* your kids to church. A wise father will take his family to church and become involved in the ministry there.

Take the Lead

If you're a father, consider how God has given you the distinct privilege of guiding those little lives toward adulthood. You've been called by God to the ministry of fatherhood. With that calling comes encouraging, inspiring, and pouring into them, and discerning their attitudes and proclivities while trying to constantly direct them toward loving and serving our Savior.

While this task might seem ominous, realize God will not call you to anything He isn't ready to help you accomplish. You're not alone in this ministry of fatherhood if you ask God for His help.

Since you are the one who should oversee the spiritual development and welfare of your family, you need to have a good idea of what it looks like to lead your family in spiritual matters. Ephesians 5:23 clearly lays out the husband's role as the "head of the wife, as also Christ is head of the church." What is Christ's example as our head? Jesus rules His church with selfless love, mercy, kindness, and grace. Your goal should be to rule your own family in the same way.

Think about the type of leader you are. In our eighteen years in youth ministry, the number one thing that drove kids from Christian homes and away from the church was hypocrisy they observed in their parents. If your walk with Christ is not genuine, your kids will know and they will likely rebel against your leadership and your biblical values.

When you're flying off the handle at your kids for not doing something you asked them to do, check your motivation. Ask yourself, "Why am I making this demand? And why am I willing to sin to get it?"

Your kids will likely emulate your behavior, even if they resent it. Weird, I know. Here's an example: If you are modeling to your family that yelling at their mom is the normal way to react, you can expect them to learn this behavior is acceptable in the way they treat their mother, their siblings, and one day, their own families.

My son Brandon recently gave me my grandson Ledger. The other day Brandon was telling me how he was changing Ledger's diaper and the little guy was screaming, kicking, crying, and generally being unhappy. Brandon calmly bent down and whispered in Ledger's ear, "You are alive because of me. I clothe you, feed you, and give you a place to live. I do everything for you. Why would you resist me when I'm just trying to help you?" (Ledger is only nine months old, but I feel the sentiment.)

All at once Brandon said he had the overwhelming thought that God says the same thing to him: "I clothe you. I care for you more than you know. I have given you life. I sustain you. Why would you ever fight against Me when I know what is best for you?"

As fathers, you and I both have experienced how our children don't really understand all we do for them, right? If you're like me, you would do anything in your power to help your child grow to be the person you see they have the potential to become. In the same way, God cares for you and is ready to help you become the man, and father, He wants you to be. That kind of struck me; how about you? Recognize you are not the source for your success as a father—God is. Do you see how remembering this could go a long way in giving you courage to lead your family?

You will never be more influential than when
you lead your family from your knees.

You will never be more influential than when you lead your family from your knees. Never underestimate the power of praying for your children and your marriage. Interceding for your kids' salvation, praying for God to guide their walk with Christ and for them to mature in their faith, is one of the greatest gifts you can give to your family. And God promises "the effective, fervent prayer of a righteous man avails much" (James 5:16). Will you be that man?

From a Wife's Perspective
A Word from Rhonda

Are we the only ones who found raising toddlers and teens increased the stress in our marriage relationship? I remember begging Steve to let me have a baby, and then after our first child was born with colic, I remember thinking, *Nobody told me how hard this was gonna be.*

The incessant crying coupled with Steve and me having differing opinions of how to soothe the child were circumstances I hadn't expected.

When we realized how ill-prepared we were as parents, rather than allowing the stress to undermine our relationship, we looked for godly mentors to give us sound advice for our parenting and our relationship. For these godly mentors we are forever grateful, as their insights, prayers, and encouragement helped us become the parents we had hoped we would be. And I am confident that finding godly mentors will do the same for you and your marriage.

Together Steve and I have raised four children (three biological and our eldest son, Tony, whom God brought to our family when he was 15 years old). Amidst the years of tweens and teens, Steve and I once again found ourselves in uncharted waters. Standing together as a united front for our kids was sometimes hard, and yet it gave them a sense of security they really needed as they grew up. And the same will be true for your children.

As a husband, know how much your wife needs you to help her raise those little people in your home. Even when she seems like she's got it all handled, realize she gets tired, overwhelmed, unsure, and likely struggles with mom-guilt (we all do). Telling your wife you're proud of her and that she's doing a good job, praying for her, and stepping in when the kiddos are making her crazy will likely pour into her the strength she needs while dealing with the daily pressures of motherhood. And don't be surprised if she sees you as her knight in armor too!

Together, watch chapter 4 video at
RhondaStoppe.com/marriage-mentor

Thinking It Through

Is parenting causing stress in your marriage relationship? Do you find yourself tempted to take sides with your kids to gang up against your spouse?

Realize that your children's security lies in the health of your marriage relationship, so any division they see in your marriage will sow seeds of insecurity in your kids. Even if they are the ones trying to drive the wedge, if you allow your child to manipulate or coerce you to fight with each other, your actions will undermine the foundation of the very place they should feel most safe.

Most parents will agree that they would do just about anything to help their kids lead a fulfilling life. Realize how working together to grow the love in your marriage will give your kids security and truly help them reach their potential.

Living It Out

Jesus said, "Whoever hears these sayings of Mine, and *does* them, I will liken him to a wise man who built his house on the rock" (Matthew 7:24, italics added).

You get one shot at this parenting thing—one! So make sure your foundation is strongly grounded in obedience to God's ways for your life. In the Bible God gives clear instructions and resources to help you succeed in the ministry of parenting—and marriage.

As a couple, talk about ways you and your spouse will build your family upon biblical principles. Take time to consider godly couples you know. Talk about what it is you admire about the couples and what you'd like to emulate. Decide to make friends with couples whose marriages have grown stronger during their years of raising kids. That's what we did when we were young parents, and we never regretted it.

Friendships with those older couples were both fun and life changing because we learned practical insights from people who had walked ahead of us on the path we were trodding. Titus chapter 2 instructs the older to mentor the younger, so following this godly principle is God's plan to strengthen your marriage and equip you for this incredible mission of parenthood.

The Grass Is Not Greener on the Other Side

THE GRASS IS GREENER WHERE IT'S WATERED

In this day of quick divorces and remarriages, lifelong relationships are all too few. Sadly, statistics generally show that around half of those who promise "Till death do us part" will never celebrate a fiftieth wedding anniversary, let alone a twenty-fifth.

When Your Husband Lets You Down

So what's the problem? Why are people so quick to abandon their vows to seek happiness in the arms of another? When couples are blissfully engaged to be married, betrayal is the furthest thing from their minds. But after they tie the knot and the years go by, the grass starts to look greener elsewhere. How is it that so many marriages are ruined because the husband or wife falls in love with someone else? And what can you do to ensure this doesn't happen to your marriage?

First, realize that women are not usually tempted to fantasize about leaving their husband for another man unless they feel like their husband repeatedly does not measure up to their expectations. The danger lies in allowing your disappointment to cause you to think, *I would be happier married to someone else.*

Whenever your husband lets you down, you most likely feel betrayed. When I use the word *betrayed*, I'm not talking about your husband having an affair with another woman, which is the ultimate betrayal. Rather, I am referring to the everyday disappointments that make you feel as though your husband is being disloyal to you. Some common examples of such betrayals are:

- when your husband vents about you on the phone to his mother
- when he spent an excessive amount of money on a frivolous item without telling you
- when he looks too intently at another woman
- when he looks at pornography
- when he makes comments to embarrass or undermine you in front of others

---

Settle in your mind how you plan to respond with forgiveness *before* an infraction occurs.

Preparing, in advance, to deal with these types of disloyalty will allow you to determine how you will handle feelings of betrayal *before* they happen. Now, I am not saying you should watch your husband in a way that suggests you don't trust him. Rather, settle in your mind how you plan to respond with forgiveness *before* an infraction occurs. And be ready to offer the same grace to your husband that you would want from him in the times that you disappoint him. If you are not prepared with a response and forgiveness, then you are more likely to deal with your disappointment irrationally. And this is when many wives begin to believe the myth "I would be happier married to someone else." Beware, for if you toy with this idea for too long, you will invite Satan to wreak havoc in your life. The devil knows that if he can get you to dream about a happier life with another man, he will have gained a foothold toward destroying your marriage. Don't give him that chance (see 2 Corinthians 2:11; Ephesians 4:27).

In the face of your husband's everyday betrayals, you have choices to make. You can either be ill-prepared for the letdown and withdraw emotionally, or you can choose to cover the betrayal with love — God's love.

How you respond will either create an emotional distance in your relationship or deepen your love for one another. You will find strength and peace to cover your disappointment with grace when you fall to your knees and seek the One who will never betray you.

The Grass May Look Greener, but It's Full of Thorns

When you become friends with happily married couples, you can learn from their example how to have a joyful union.

I come from a long line of broken marriages. So, as a young bride, I wanted to learn the secret to a happy and lasting marriage. For help, I looked to a number of godly women in our church whose marriages I wanted to emulate. When you become friends with happily married couples, you can learn from their example how to have a joyful union. Can you think of at least one godly couple whom you would like to emulate? If not, pray for the Lord to lead you to some.

When we were younger, most of the couples Steve and I spent time with were older than we were. And the wives in these marriages took seriously the instruction in Titus 2 for older women to teach younger women how to love their husbands. This made them great mentors for me.

When I would ask these women, "What is the key to a happy marriage?" I was surprised at their answers. The overall message I gleaned from these Titus 2 women was this:

> The real secret to a happy marriage is not in how much you
> love your husband but how much you love Christ. God

created us to worship Him. When you make it a priority to worship God through quiet time with the Lord in Bible study, prayer, repentance, and obedience to His will, you will find your joy, identity, and sense of well-being in your relationship with your Creator. When this happens, you will not feel the need to find your worth in your relationship with your spouse, and you will never be tempted to look to another man to fulfill you either.

God created you with a need to be loved and to feel significant. But He never intended for you to fulfill those desires through marriage—or through any relationship with a person. Rather, God wants to fill the longings of your heart with Himself. The problem is that sin stole away mankind's desire for intimacy with the Creator. And now, because of sin in your heart—and mine—we focus on self and struggle with self-worship. In this state of self-love, you are susceptible to think, *I deserve to be happy* and to believe Satan's lie, "I would be happier with someone else." In this vulnerable state, when one romantic relationship fails to make you feel complete, there is a temptation to replace it with another one.

The only way to guard against having a distorted sense of love and self-worth is to have a healthy personal relationship with Jesus. Again, that involves growing your love for Him through prayer, spending time in Bible study, and fellowshipping with other Christians who are truly seeking a more intimate walk with Christ. When you determine to find your joy in Christ, you will be set free from looking to others to fill the void only God can satisfy.

Eight Insights We Learned from Happily Married Couples

Here are eight practical ways you can cultivate a happy marriage:

1. Have Realistic Expectations

One reason people become unhappy with their marriage is because the relationship doesn't turn out to be all they had expected. Did you think your husband would be the answer to all your hopes for happily-ever-after? If so, at some point after the honeymoon was over, you came to realize you had married a normal human being and not the Prince Charming you imagined him to be.

My "aha moment" came during our honeymoon when my brand-new husband proceeded to use the bathroom in front of me. I was shocked. I mean, I knew this big hunk of a man relieved himself, but it never occurred to me he would do it in my presence!

The sooner you realize you and your husband are both imperfect people, the better you will be prepared to cover with grace the times you let one another down.

2. Your Husband Is Not Like You

You don't have to be married for too long to discover your husband is not like you. All too often, couples attempt to define unity in marriage as "sameness." But unity isn't sameness.

For example, one way men and women differ from each other is the way they respond to discord. In conflict, a woman will generally pull away, secretly hoping her husband will come after her to show her how much he cares. But most men require time to process a heated conversation. They often need to distance themselves from the situation and think through what was said. This is why, after a disagreement, your husband may go out to the garage to work on a task. While he is contemplating his own feelings, trying to understand how you are feeling, and possibly looking for a way to resolve the conflict, it would be easy for you to interpret his pulling away as rejection or a lack of concern for you and your feelings.

So don't be quick to assume your husband's retreat means that he doesn't care. And learn how to give your husband the space he needs to come back and have a rational conversation—when he is ready.

Remember, unity in marriage does not mean you have to see eye to eye with your husband on every detail of life. In his book *What Did You Expect?* author Paul David Tripp says,

> Unity in marriage is not the result of sameness...God has designed that you will be married to someone different

from you. Unity is, rather, the result of what husband and wife do in the face of inevitable differences…The more you look at your spouse and see the imprint of God's fingers… the more you will be able to resist the temptation to try to remake him in your own image…The more you see divine beauty…in the differences between you, the less you will be irritated by them.[1]

When you begin to celebrate God's imprint on your husband, you will be prepared to implement the next insight I learned from happy couples:

3. Think the Best About Your Husband

I know that in chapter 3 we already talked about dwelling on your husband's good qualities, but it bears repeating in this context. Remind yourself regularly of the qualities you love about your husband. And resist the temptation to compare him to the "ideal husband" you dream of having. Wouldn't you want your husband to do the same for you?

Even with deliberate effort toward resisting the temptation to compare, married couples will often lean toward viewing one another through a negative lens. If thinking the best about each other is not yet a habit within your marriage, someone has to take the first step. Let that someone be you.

Many couples I have talked to will admit to having had a mediocre marriage—or even a bad one—until one of them determined to stop comparing their spouse to the person they wished he or she would be. In so doing, their newfound habit of thinking positive thoughts spilled over into affirming words and kind service to their spouse. More often than not, the actions of one spouse not only turned the marriage around, but in many instances even saved the marriage.

4. Be Kind to One Another

Are you kind? I don't mean are you nice to the mailman or the bagger at the grocery store. It's easy to be kind to people you only see for a few minutes each day. But in general, do you have a kind disposition?

Is kindness your default mode, or do you have to force yourself not to lash out when you are offended? Maybe a better question to ask would be this: Does your husband think you are kind?

Ephesians 4:32 says, "Be kind one to another." This is a command, not a suggestion. And yet wouldn't you agree there are times that being kind is not the easiest response? And if you have little ones at home, lack of sleep alone can have a negative influence upon your attempts to remain kind. One marriage expert says women in their thirties (when most women have small children) go through what he refers to as "the unfriendly years."[2] Can I get a witness? As a stay-at-home mom, I recall being tired, overworked, and "underpaid." *Unfriendly* would certainly define the way I sometimes treated my husband in those days. (I remember thinking, *He gets to go to work every day in an air-conditioned office and have lunch with grown-ups, while I'm chasing after kids and up to my elbows in laundry.*)

Have you ever struggled with this type of thinking? Would you characterize yourself as unfriendly to your husband? If while reading this you find yourself resentful — for whatever reason — realize that holding on to resentment will only end up hurting your marriage. Whatever the situation or your circumstances, if you make an extra effort to be kind to your husband now, you will enjoy the benefit of a happier marriage as time goes on.

The seeds of kindness Steve and I planted during the chaotic years of raising children have borne fruit, and today we find ourselves in the midst of a delightful empty-nest season. By contrast, I know many wives who were unkind to their husbands because they harbored an unforgiving attitude and resentment over their husband's lack of help when the kids were little, only to reap a broken marriage when the children grew up and left home.

5. Refuse to Fantasize About Being Married to Someone Else

A major threat to a happy marriage is the temptation to believe you married the wrong person.

Watching soap operas or romantic movies can easily lead to a restless heart within a woman. After her own life fell apart, a friend of mine told me, "Whenever you teach women, warn them not to watch soap operas. I used to watch them for hours and wish my life was as interesting as the lives of the people on the show. When the drama visited my own marriage, it nearly destroyed me. The lifestyle I thought would spark a new fire brought devastation and destruction."

When times get hard—and they will—allowing yourself to daydream about what it would be like to escape the hardship will only invite trouble into your marriage. If you are looking up old boyfriends on the Internet or dreaming about what life would be like if you were married to a different man, you are already in the process of undermining the foundation of your marriage.

In the Sermon on the Mount, Jesus told the story of the foolish man who built his house upon the sand (Matthew 7:26-27). Building your hopes for a happy marriage with someone other than your husband is certainly foolish. And when the storms of life come, your house will come crashing down around you.

6. Your Husband Is Not Your Enemy

In times of strife, remind yourself that your husband is not your enemy. Your real adversary is the devil, who is a roaring lion seeking to devour you—and your marriage.[3] The enemy is fully aware of the devastating effect a broken marriage can have on your kids, so realize he will work to stir up conflict in your marriage in an attempt to turn your children away from Christ.

Recently a rattlesnake found its way into our house. Crazy? I know! Steve had stepped over the snake as he walked out onto the porch, and the thing slithered right into our home. Steve called for me to come and keep an eye on the snake while he ran to get a shovel to kill it.

"Me? You want *me* to keep watch?" I shouted.

As he ran out the door, he explained the importance of keeping an eye on the snake so it didn't get lost somewhere in the house.

Soon Steve returned with a shovel and cut off the head of this four-foot-long rattling adversary and we were safe. *My hero!*

What if when the snake entered the house I began to blame Steve for leaving the door open? What if I refused to come and keep watch out of fear or resentment? You see where I am going with this? In the same way Steve and I worked together to stand against the awful creature wreaking havoc on our home, it is important that you draw together in the fight against Satan when he slithers into your lives.

And just as Steve asked me to keep watch while he ran to grab a weapon, the Bible instructs us, "Be sober, be vigilant; because your adversary the devil walks about like a roaring lion, seeking whom he may devour" (1 Peter 5:8).

When you realize Satan comes to steal, kill, and destroy, you will know that it's the tempter who is your enemy, not your husband, and you'll be ready to stand together in the fight against your foe.

7. Love Christ More Than You Love Your Husband

I know we have discussed this several times in this book, but I cannot stress enough this key principle: when you determine to grow more deeply in love with Christ, you will find your worth in your relationship to Him. When this happens, you will not look to your husband to meet the needs only God can fill. When you live to love Jesus, His love for your husband will spill out of your heart. And your heart will become joyfully satisfied with your husband.

One marriage counselor offers this insight: "Love is being unwilling to ask your spouse to be the source of your identity, meaning and purpose, or inner sense of well-being, while refusing to be the source of his."[4]

8. Determine That Divorce Will Never Be an Option

If ever you think leaving your marriage is the answer to your problems, remind yourself: *wherever you go, there you are.* This means whatever struggles you may be having, realize you are half of the problem. If you choose to leave a difficult marriage, you can be certain you'll take all your unresolved issues into your next relationship as well. And while we are on this subject, let's talk a bit more about the consequences of divorce.

The Effects of Divorce

Whenever couples have built a distance between themselves through hurtful words, unwillingness to forgive, or neglect, they may start to believe divorce is the only answer. Sadly, we live in a culture that thinks the goal of life is happiness at all costs, so divorce has become a very common choice, even among Christians. However, you can be sure the happiness you are seeking will elude you as you face the devastating fallout that comes with a divorce.

Over the course of our years in youth work, my husband and I observed again and again the stress that raising a teen can have on a marriage (which helped give us wisdom for when we raised our own teens). Some of the parents we knew chose to abandon their marriage vows when the times got rough—only to find themselves facing a whole new set of problems that come with raising teenagers in a broken home.

The children's pastor of our church told me, "In almost 20 years of working with kids, I have observed that the most harmful decision a parent can make for their child is to get a divorce." (Please understand that this statement does not hold true if there is abuse in the home.)

I have heard women say, "Our kids will be happier if they are not exposed to our constant fighting." Sadly, after the divorce, I have heard these same women regretfully admit how deeply their children were wounded by the breakup. Here are some heartbreaking realities that children of divorce will likely face:

- Mom and Dad are less focused on their children as they work to establish their new single life. Whether the parents are focused on career, dating, or dealing with their own hurt after the divorce, kids inevitably suffer the consequences.

- One or both of the parents remarry, which introduces step-children or siblings from the new marriage into the family. When this happens, your kids will struggle with feeling overlooked or less valued by their biological parents. Then there is the all-too-common threat of kids being sexually abused by a stepparent or stepsibling.

- Children who grow up in broken homes deal with deep-seated insecurity issues that often lead to them repeating the cycle of divorce in their own marriages.

Over the many years I have mentored women, I've learned that one major contributor to a woman's distrust of her husband's loyalty is her own parents' divorce. So don't deceive yourself into believing your broken marriage won't have any effect on your children's marriages. When my parents divorced after 30 years of marriage, I was well into my twenties and happily married with two children of my own. Even though I was an adult, their divorce shook my security in ways I never would have dreamed. Without a doubt, my parents' divorce is one of the most grievous experiences I have ever endured.

Till Death Do Us Part

Can you think of an older couple you know who has stuck it out through the bad times? A couple you would like to emulate? My husband's parents, Bill and Eleanore, were just such a couple. My mother-in-law was deeply in love with "Willie," as she called him. And I was captivated by their adoration for each other.

At first glance, you would think they never had any struggles in their marriage. But the reality was that Bill and Eleanore had weathered a number of difficult storms in life. For example, Bill was deployed to Korea not long after their marriage. While he was away, Eleanore suffered alone through a tragic miscarriage. In the first five years of their marriage, the couple silently grieved over their inability to conceive. So you can imagine their relief—and elation—when Steve was born. And then three years later, God blessed them with another son, Daniel.

When Steve and I were dating, he used to tell me his parents *never* fought. I didn't believe him. I would say, "Every married couple fights. Your parents are just hiding it from you and your brother."

But through the years I came to discover that Steve's perception of his parents' relationship was spot-on. The two genuinely adored one another. When life had been hard, rather than looking for a "better life" with someone else, they pressed into their relationship with Christ—and into one another.

Bill and Eleanore's devotion for each other shone the brightest when Eleanore was diagnosed with Alzheimer's disease. The first thing she forgot was how to play the piano. Playing music for her church had been her great delight. You can imagine her sorrow when she couldn't remember how to play her favorite hymns. Bill grieved quietly for his bride.

For a decade, Bill devoted himself to Eleanore's care. Many nights I would hear him sobbing on the front porch as my husband held his dad in his arms. After a number of years, the stress of taking care of Eleanore was taking a toll on Bill's health, so we suggested he put her in an assisted-care facility—to which Bill replied, "She is my sweetheart. I would *never* dream of leaving her care to someone else."

Talk about love. My kids and I were privy to watching true love lived out through Bill and Eleanore. Even when "Ellie" (as Bill called her) didn't remember who Bill was, he continued to take care of her. He even went so far as to sell their home, quit his job, and move into a house on our ranch so he could care for his love full-time.

The love demonstrated by my in-laws has left a lasting impression upon me, their children, and their grandchildren. Jesus said, "Greater love has no one than this, than to lay down one's life for his friends" (John 15:13). Steve's father certainly personified this kind of selfless love until the day his beloved Eleanore passed on into eternity.

Have you ever considered the story you are writing with your life? This generation is desperate for love stories like those in this book. Won't you join the ranks of Vi and Curt (from chapter 1), who waltzed in each other's arms until Curt's final breath, and Bill and Eleanore, whose undying love withstood a failing mind?

When you learn that true joy and satisfaction are not found in a perfect marriage with a perfect person but rather come from your relationship with Christ, you will learn the secret to a happy marriage. I pray you will apply the biblical principles laid out in this book so you can build a no-regrets marriage. And through your example, may your children and grandchildren learn the secret to a happy marriage.

From a Husband's Perspective
A Word from Steve

After reading about my parents, I had a hard time writing this conclusion to Rhonda's chapter. Remembering how much my mom and dad loved one another brings about emotions that are strangely sad, yet joyful. Growing up under my parents' example, I learned what God intended unconditional love between a husband and wife to look like. Because my parents did not attempt to find their identity, acceptance, or value in each other, but rather in their relationship with Christ, they learned how to love one another selflessly. Even when my mom didn't remember who my dad was because of her Alzheimer's, my father continued to love and serve her—all the while grieving the loss of who she had once been.

For you as a believer, finding your identity, acceptance, or value in your spouse—or any other earthly relationship—is always a dangerous path to tread. You will certainly be disappointed if you attempt to establish your worth based on your husband's view of you because at some point your husband will let you down, and your perceived security will be shattered. It is in this place of disappointment that a woman may be tempted to look outside of her marriage relationship to another man to find her worth.

Galatians 2:20 says, "I have been crucified with Christ; it is no longer I who live, but Christ lives in me; and the life which I now live in the flesh I live by faith in the Son of God, who loved me and gave Himself for me." As much as Rhonda loves, accepts, and affirms me, she can never do for me all that Christ has done. And the same is true for you and your spouse.

Instead of looking to your husband to make you feel treasured, make it your goal to die to yourself daily. And live by faith in the Son of God, who loved you so much He gave His life so that you could be made alive in Christ. Learn to remind yourself daily, through Scripture, just how precious you are to God. When you do, you will let your husband off the hook for being the source of your self-worth, and guard yourself from the temptation to look elsewhere for happiness.

Make no mistake—I am not saying you shouldn't want your husband to say and do things that make you feel loved. First Peter 3:7 tells us Christian men are to live with our wives according to understanding. That means God expects husbands to try to meet their wives' emotional needs. But know that we men often need help with understanding what you need from us. If your husband is to try to learn what actions he can take to affirm his love for you, he will need you to coach him, because, left to ourselves, more often than not we guys will get it wrong. And trying to figure out what our wives need at any given moment can be a rather intimidating task for *all* men. So if you find your husband not doing enough to make you happy, don't ever believe the lie that another man would understand your needs better—because it's just not true.

Accepting the fact that the ultimate goal of your life is to bring glory and honor to God is the first step you can take toward building a marriage that stands the tests of time.

In a marriage, both the husband and the wife bear the responsibility when they wrongly expect to find their worth in the way their spouse treats them. Accepting the fact that the ultimate goal of your life is to bring glory and honor to God is the first step you can take toward building a marriage that stands the tests of time.

Wives, listen to chapter 5 audio "The Grass Is Not Greener" at **RhondaStoppe.com/marriage-mentor**

Man to Man

There have been a number of times men have come into my office confessing they have had thoughts of leaving their wives for someone else who has grabbed their attention. Fortunately, most of those men had not physically acted on their impulses.

But in their minds they had come up with a list of reasons they wanted to share with me to justify why they thought they would be happier with this other woman.

I remember one man in particular came in wanting me to talk him off the ledge, so to speak. He was struggling with temptation and was genuinely looking for sound advice. When wrestling with the idea of acting on an impulse, men often do not look ahead down the road to weigh out the consequences of their actions. So I had this man take a mental walk with me down that road. I began, "Let's look at what the rest of your life will be like should you decide to act on your impulse. Then you'll be better equipped to decide if that is the decision you want to make."

We talked about what would happen to his family should he decide to leave his wife. I helped him consider what it would be like when his wife eventually found someone else to love her, care for her, and meet her needs—the way he had once promised to. I reminded him of how devastated and insecure his wife would likely be if he left. Which would make her vulnerable to possibly choosing a new husband who was a "scum-sucking-maggot" (yes, I used those words). I said, "Just think what life for your wife and kids would be like if this became their plight."

I went on, "And if you're truly a believer and you leave your family for another woman, God promises to make you miserable in your rebellion. So don't think you can sin against God and still be happy."

As the man pondered my words, I saw a glimmer of hope that his love for his wife and his family was not beyond repair. Fortunately, for this man the reality check was enough to wake him up from the fantasy of what it would be like to be adored by some sweet young thing he'd been flirting with at the office.

Our conversation was the first of many, but in the end the man came to repentance over his longing for something more than what God had blessed him with. And with his repentance came a renewed commitment to loving his wife, which transformed his marriage.

In over 30 years of ministry, I can attest to the fact that the circumstances this man was in are not farfetched. If you are a man, then you will likely be tempted at some point to wonder if you would be happier with someone else. Maybe you'll never act on the temptation—and I pray that you don't. But let me walk you down the path of what I've seen happen when a husband forsakes the wife of his youth.

Very few women who are left by their husbands remain single. Most often they marry again. Can you imagine another man tucking your children into bed? And how would you feel if your kids came to see you on your weekend of visitation crying over how harsh or neglectful their stepfather was to them? Or maybe your kids won't want to come see you at all, because their stepdad is amazing and they prefer him over you as they wrestle with resentment toward you for abandoning them.

Let's say you married your new wife. And let's imagine she's all you hoped she would be (although from my limited experience I sincerely doubt that will happen). But let's say it does and she's great. Now what? You'll go on with your life, possibly have more kids with wife number two. And where does that leave the kids you have now? It leaves them wondering where they fit into your new life.

God says He hates divorce for a reason. It leaves a generation of children who feel rejected, forgotten, and passed over as they become the casualties of their parents' selfish actions. (If you're reading this and you're the father who is married to another woman and is not spending time with the kids from your previous marriage, rather than recoil in guilt, step up in faith that God can heal your relationship with your children and even with your ex-wife. Be ready to ask your kids to forgive you and then look to God to help you be a godly father to your kids—despite the divorce.)

Staying together for the sake of the kids is not the point.

While your kids will be better off if you remain faithful to their mother, what they really need is to see you so in love with their mom that they're secure in knowing you'll *never* leave them.

Think About *What* You Think About

The first advice I have for you is to think about what you think about. The next time you start to think the grass is greener on the other side, realize the grass is green where you water it. Water the soil in your marriage and it will flourish.

I know what I'm talking about. For many years I've raised livestock on our ranch. I still have to chuckle when I see a cow crane its neck through a barbed fence to reach that one green blade of grass that she is convinced will taste better than the green grass in her pen.

In the same way, men who ponder how delicious the forbidden fruit of another woman might be are missing the delightful marriage they could be enjoying.

The next time your mind starts to imagine what it would be like with someone else, take that thought captive to the obedience of Christ and recognize the seduction is coming from your flesh and from the enemy who wants to kill, steal, and destroy all of the blessings God would have for you and your family (see John 10:10; 2 Corinthians 10:5).

Think About *When* You Think About

Stop looking to this world as the end of all things, and think about when you will spend eternity with the Lord. People who don't know Christ have a "go for the gusto" mentality because they have no hope of a heavenly home. If you're a Christian, it is time to start viewing life with a heavenly perspective. God's goal in saving you is not to give you a happy life free from trials. Unfortunately in our self-centered and entitled society it is easy to believe God's goal for saving you was simply to give you an easy life now and then bless you with heaven when you die. Instead, it is important to realize God is more interested in molding your character to be more like His Son so He can use your life for His kingdom purposes.

While heaven is the promise we look forward to, it is God's plan to glorify Himself through your life on earth by whatever means He deems necessary.

When you learn to take your focus off of the good life you think you deserve to live and instead put your eyes on eternity and the reward that awaits those who live in obedience to His commands, your focus will become less on yourself and temporary satisfaction. And you'll live the abundant life of obedience to Christ while storing up eternal treasures in heaven, where one day you will hear, "Well done."

In light of eternity, what is at stake if you forsake the wife of your youth? The shortsighted decision to leave this wife with whom God has united you as one flesh would cause you to be ineffective for the cross of Christ — *ineffective*!

Because of selfishness, your Christian testimony would be ruined. Your actions would be telling folks — including your children — that God doesn't expect us to endure through hardship and struggle. Rather than persevering so that Christ might be glorified, your example would say you preferred the easy out. This action would not shine for Christ; it would tout a self-serving existence that puts your happiness first and brings dishonor to God.

Think About *Who* You Think About

I see three people you should think about when you're tempted to believe you'd be happier with someone else:

First, consider the men who have gone before you. I know men who left their wife for another woman, only to later regret their decision. After a time, these men came to realize their happiness would not be found in a different wife, and they now live with regret.

Second, Hebrews 12:2 instructs believers, "Looking unto Jesus, the author and finisher of our faith, who for the joy that was set before Him endured the cross, despising the shame, and has sat down at the right hand of the throne of God." When your marriage is not measuring up to your expectations and you're tempted to think you could be happier with someone else, look to the example of Jesus, who endured great cost for the joy that was set before Him, and think about the joy that is to come for those who endure.

Finally, you should think about your wife. Think on the good things (Philippians 4:8). Every day remember something good about your wife and dwell on that memory. Then find something new to delight about in her and think about that.

Stop playing over in your mind those things that irritate or bug you. Determine to love your woman the way she needs to be loved, and that begins in your mind (we talked about this in chapter 3). Ask God to help you think the best about her, and pray that she will think the best of you. Like you did when you were dating, and from this day forward, when you think about your wife, try to think on whatever is good, right, and honorable, and you won't be tempted to look for greener grass elsewhere.

Does This Stuff Really Work?

You may be thinking, *This is all pie-in-the-sky stuff. That doesn't really work in real life. And you don't know my wife.* You're right, I don't know your wife or your situation, but I do know my God. I have watched Him turn hearts of husbands back toward their wives when they implement these steps.

Learning to combat wrong thinking when you are tempted, focusing on the good things about your marriage, and viewing your life in light of eternity will lead you to a deeper satisfaction with your wife, strengthen you against temptation, provide security to your kids, and most importantly honor Christ.

When you choose to live with a heavenly perspective, you will live in a way that stores up for yourself treasures in heaven, and one day you will hear from the Father, "Well done, good and faithful servant" (Matthew 25:21).

From a Wife's Perspective
A Word from Rhonda

I imagine I speak for most wives when I tell you how aware we are that there are women out there who would love to steal our man away from us. It happens all the time. Gentlemen, beware: *good guys have affairs*. If it could happen to them, it can happen to you.

I have dear friends, married to wonderful men, who have wept sorrowfully when they learned their husbands were unfaithful. My heart broke one day as a young married man shared with Steve how, after he had given in to his fantasy to be with another woman, he sat in his car weeping bitterly over his sin.

More than one man has tearfully explained to Steve how they never meant to act on their fantasy of infidelity. But the more they played over in their mind the idea of intimacy with another woman, the less wrong it seemed—until one day they fell to a sin they never actually meant to commit.

That's how sin works. James 1:15 describes it this way: "When desire has conceived, it gives birth to sin; and sin, when it is full-grown, brings forth death."

Steve covered some great stuff in this section. I pray you take to heart and apply the principles he shared with you. I pray that God gives you His heart for your wife and your marriage so that your children will grow up in the security of your loving home, and so that God can do through you all that He has planned before the foundations of this world.

Together, watch chapter 5 video at
RhondaStoppe.com/marriage-mentor

Thinking It Through

When the apostle Peter confidently proclaimed to Jesus that he would never deny Him, Jesus responded, "Satan has asked for you, that he may sift you as wheat. But I have prayed for you, that your faith should not fail" (Luke 22:31-32).

You can know that Satan would love to sift like wheat your marriage and family. What can you learn from Jesus' response to help you and your spouse stay faithful and committed to one another?

Living It Out

If you have developed a habit of being unkind to one another, realize that God can help you change. James 4:2 says, "You do not have because you do not ask." So begin by seeking help from the Lord. Spend some time praying together, asking God to help you learn to respond to one another in kindness.

In this chapter Rhonda outlined eight principles we can learn from happily married couples. Discuss each insight, making note of how you will apply these principles to your own marriage. To help you build a no-regrets marriage, keep this list where you can refer to it often.

1. Have realistic expectations.

2. Your spouse is not like you.

3. Think the best about your spouse.

4. Be kind to one another.

5. Refuse to fantasize about being married to someone else.

6. Your spouse is not your enemy.

7. Love Christ more than you love your spouse.

8. Determine that divorce will never be an option.

Telling Her She's Pretty and Keeping His Attention

George Müller is well remembered as a man who rescued thousands of helpless orphaned children from the cruel streets of England. In his famous orphan houses in Bristol, he helped provide for their basic needs and gave them an education as well.

As a young man, George met the beautiful Ermegarde at a Bible study. He loved the way her curls danced around her face when she giggled. When George was convinced God was calling him to be a missionary, he shared his dream with Ermegarde, whom he intended to marry. Ermegarde turned up her nose and said, "'I could never be a missionary. Missionaries are poor...Be a lawyer, or a doctor, and leave being a missionary for other people who don't have anything better to do!' With that she stood up and stomped out of the room."[1]

After agonizing over this for several weeks, George knew he had to end his relationship with Ermegarde. Only then would he be free to follow the Lord's leading.

Later, George met Mary Groves, who was not at all like Ermegarde—either in external beauty or inner attitudes. As one biography tells it:

> The relationship blossomed, and George found himself
> in love with Mary. Such a feeling surprised him for more

than one reason. First, Mary was eight years older than he was. And second, he had not been looking for or even considering a wife. As far as he was concerned, a wife would slow him down. What if God called him to go someplace strange or remote? Could he expect a wife to follow him? And would he feel as though marriage made him a prisoner?

Although George may not have expected just any wife to follow him, there was something about Mary.[2]

Soon the two were married. Mary set up housekeeping, and a week later, all her belongings were in George's tiny home. When George saw Mary's fancy silver and china, he talked with her and asked her to sell all her treasures for their ministry. Mary responded, "Do what you think is best…and may God help us both."

A while later, when George and Mary were out walking, George said,

> "Mary, thank you for selling the things. Now there is another matter we need to talk about…It's the pew rent. I can't see how we can follow Jesus' command to treat all men equally if we give rich people the best pews."
>
> Mary said, "But, George, that's our only income…"
>
> George said, "I know it's hard, but I think it is the right thing to do."
>
> Mary said, "Do what you think is best, George. I can trust God, just like you do."
>
> George stopped and hugged his wife. Tears spilled down his cheeks. Mary had been right—marriage had not become a prison for him. Instead, it had given him a partner in the faith.[3]

Together, George and Mary chose to trust God to fully meet their needs and to give all else to ministry. It's reported that over the course of his life, nearly 1.5 million pounds passed through George's hands to provide food, shelter, and clothing for the multitudes of orphaned children in his care. He died with very little money to his name because he gave it all to ministry.

What's more, George and Mary determined never to ask any person for money to support their orphanages. They simply prayed with faith and watched God provide for their every need—sometimes at the very last possible moment. It is for this reason that George Müller is considered to be a man of incredible faith.

When Mary Müller died, George preached a short message at her funeral and quoted Psalm 119:68 (ASV): "Thou art good, and doest good." The funeral service was one of the largest Bristol had ever seen. Thousands of letters poured in from orphans whom Mary had nurtured as children.

George was comforted by the letters, but he missed Mary greatly. Though she may not have been pretty by the world's standards, George knew his wife was one of the most beautiful women this world had ever known. In her, he had found a good thing.

Beauty for God's Purpose

In the Bible, we read of women whom God worked through on account of their beauty. Queen Esther is a perfect example. The Bible says Esther was fair and beautiful (Esther 2:7). God had a purpose in her beauty, and it wasn't because He favored her. No, the Lord used Esther's looks to attract the attention of the king of Persia, who chose Esther to become his queen. This put her in the perfect position to be God's tool to help spare the people of Israel from annihilation.

Whether you are pretty in the world's estimation or you would consider yourself average, don't believe the myth "My husband would love me more if I were prettier." The truth is, a woman holds her husband's attention captive because of her inner loveliness.

So Is It Wrong to Want Your Husband to Think You Are Beautiful?

Almost every married woman wants her husband to tell her she's pretty. The trouble begins when you believe you will feel more valued if your husband makes you feel beautiful. When you start to think external beauty is what gives you value, you fail to understand your worth to your Creator. And when this happens, you become vulnerable to looking for affirmation on a human level.

Anytime Christians seek from another person what only God can give, they make the person an idol. In a marriage relationship, if you look to your husband to satisfy your desire to be treasured, he will ultimately let you down, because God never intended for your spouse to fill the void only He can fill.

God created you to find your worth and purpose in your relationship with Him alone. Listen to how much God treasures you: "In this is love, not that we loved God, but that He loved us and sent His Son to be the propitiation for our sins" (1 John 4:10). And, "See how great a love the Father has bestowed on us, that we would be called children of God; and such we are" (1 John 3:1 NASB).

A wise woman will learn to find her worth in her standing with Christ so she can delight in her husband's compliments from a pure heart. When the Lord is the delight of your heart, the kind words you receive from your husband will only add to your joy.

So is it wrong to want your husband to think you are beautiful? I don't think so. A biblical example of a husband captivated by his wife's beauty can be found in the Song of Solomon, where King Solomon refers to his beloved as "fairest among women."[4]

While it is nice to receive such affirmation from your man, just make sure you are finding your worth in your vertical relationship with God, not in the horizontal relationship with your husband. And if it turns out you are married to a man who is not complimentary like King Solomon, by God's grace you can know your worth in Christ, and you can learn to cover your husband's shortcomings with God's love. First Peter 4:8 (NASB) says, "Above all, keep fervent in your love for one another, because love covers a multitude of sins."

What If He Never Tells Me I'm Pretty?

What should you do if your husband constantly forgets to compliment you? I have heard women tell their husbands things like, "Karen's husband is so sweet. He always tells her she's pretty." In saying this, wives expect their husbands to hear, "I wish you would compliment me like Karen's husband compliments her."

Instead, what their husbands hear is this: "Wow, Karen's husband is a great guy. Why can't you be more like him?"

When your husband hears you comparing him to another man, he is not likely to try to become more like the man you have held up as an example. Rather, he is more likely to feel disrespected by you and shut down.

If you really want to help your husband understand how he can minister to you in this area, tell him. Prayerfully consider your words and your motivation before you have a heart-to-heart with him. Ask God for wisdom. James 1:5 says anyone who lacks wisdom can ask it of God, who gives it liberally and generously. Have you ever asked God to give you His wisdom before you attempted to have sensitive or difficult conversations with your husband? Try it. Asking for God's wisdom will help you speak in a God-centered way rather than a self-centered one.

After you talk to your husband, pray for God to help him understand your need. Let God do a work in his heart. Pray often, and don't expect your husband to change overnight. Be willing to remind him or even playfully nudge him to compliment you, if necessary.

First Corinthians chapter 13 is called the "love chapter" of the Bible. The passage is filled with a wonderful list of the characteristics of genuine love. In verse 7, we read that love "believes all things." That is, the most genuine kind of love *believes the best* about the other person.

So I ask you: Is your husband a goodwilled man? Is it possible he is not intentionally overlooking opportunities to affirm your beauty? Are there things you forget to do for him? When that happens, do you hope he will believe the best about you? Can you apply this same kind of mercy to your husband if he neglects or forgets to compliment you?

Don't Set Yourself Up for Disappointment

In her book *What I Wish My Mother Had Told Me About Men*, my friend Julie Gorman has this to say:

Doesn't it feel good when a man affirms you? Of course! We all crave these things—and that's what makes us vulnerable. As we search for significance and validation, God's word strongly commands, "Do not trust in princes, in mortal man, in whom there is no salvation" (Psalm 146:3 NASB).

Embracing the fallacy that a man will validate our worth positions us for heartache and disappointment.[5]

Why Do We Need to Hear We Are Beautiful?

Have you ever considered what life must have been like for Adam and Eve before they fell into sin? Talk about a honeymoon! They would have found themselves in the most romantic resort, complete with an all-inclusive food menu. They had the whole garden to themselves, and Adam had eyes only for Eve.

Before the fall, Adam and Eve's unity with one another—and their Creator—would have been absolute paradise. Because they lived in joyful union with God, His character would have been reflected in all areas of their lives. Their love for one another would have been completely selfless and God-centered. They would have loved perfectly because they were a perfect reflection of the Creator's love.

But once sin entered into the world, not only was Adam and Eve's fellowship with God broken, but for the first time, their total unity with one another was violated as well. What a heartbreak this must have been!

After they fell into sin, God questioned Adam about what he had done, and he blamed his wife.[6] Oh wow! In that moment, Eve would have realized the honeymoon was definitely over. Can you imagine how hurt Eve must have been?

From that day on, the heart of mankind became desperately sick and wicked.[7] In her book *Idols of the Heart*, Elyse Fitzpatrick gives this insight:

> Our hearts, the fount from which all sin flows (Matthew 12:34), have ceased to be God-centered and have become self-centered. Rather than living to reflect God for His

glory, man lives for his own glory, seeking happiness in his own reflection…Rather than desiring to enjoy the beauty and order of creation for God's glory, they deify outward appearances. They long for others to worship their beauty and creativity. They make a god of their home, clothing, car or anything that reflects their glory, beauty, or worth.[8]

Elyse addresses a very real tendency we have to be self-focused rather than God-focused. When any desire becomes so important we would sin to get it, we can know that desire has become an idol.

So What Should I Do?

By now you may be asking, "How can I balance being God-centered with wanting my husband to think I am pretty? And how can I discern if my desire is sinful?"

Ask yourself this question: "If my husband does not make me feel beautiful, do I resent him?" Resenting your husband is a sin. If his making you feel pretty is so important to you that you will sin to get it, then you can know you are idolizing your desire.

You will never see yourself more clearly
than through the lens of Scripture.

Through Bible study, the Holy Spirit can help you discern your motives. You will never see yourself more clearly than through the lens of Scripture.[9] So you must be in the Word on a daily basis, asking God to help you become God-centered rather than self-centered. In this way you can discern your sin and confess it.[10] As one Christian writer observed, "It is hypocritical to pray for victory over our sins yet be careless in our intake of the Word of God."[11]

Maybe I Shouldn't Try So Hard

Now, before you are tempted to think trying to be pretty for your husband is somehow "unspiritual," I want to give you some insight into how a husband appreciates a wife who cares about how she looks.

In her book *For Women Only*, Shaunti Feldhahn talks about an anonymous survey she conducted with more than one thousand men. Here's what men said about their wives making an effort to look pretty:

> In a way this issue for men is like the romance issue for us. Maybe it shouldn't matter whether our husbands ever put one jot of effort into romancing us. But it does. We love him regardless, but it doesn't salve the empty wistfulness we feel or the pain we may suffer wondering why on earth our man doesn't see that this is so important to us.
>
> Guys feel the same way on the issue of our appearance—or at least our effort. It is critical that we acknowledge that this male desire is both real and legitimate.
>
> [Another man said,] "I want to be proud of my wife. Every man has this innate competition with other men, and our wives are a part of that. Every man wants other men to think that he did well."

Now, hold on, before you translate the comments from those men to mean, "We want you all to be skinny and look great in a bikini," listen to what a majority of men said:

> Sometimes I'll meet a man whose wife is overweight—but she takes care of herself. She puts some effort into her appearance. She dresses neatly, or does her makeup and hair. If she is comfortable in her own skin and is confident, you don't notice the extra pounds. I look at that husband and think, *He did well.*[12]

The Secret to Keeping His Attention

We all envy the couples who seem captivated by each other. You know who they are. They catch each other's gaze across the room and give a flirtatious wink. Who is this wife who seems to hold her husband's attention in spite of children, financial difficulties, and those extra pounds she has held on to since the babies came?

Don't you want to *be* that woman? What is her secret? How has this wife managed to keep her husband's attention, and what can you learn from her?

First Timothy 2 encourages godly women to focus less on adorning themselves externally and instead to live in a manner that professes godliness. God's secret to capturing your husband's affection for a lifetime is for you to be devoted to developing your inner beauty.

An Example of Inner Beauty

A wonderful example of a woman who exuded beauty from within is Ruth. The Bible tells us Ruth lived in Moab. There, she was married to a Jewish man who evidently died at a relatively young age. When Ruth's widowed mother-in-law, Naomi, decided to return to her homeland of Israel, the recently widowed Ruth was determined to go with her. In doing this, Ruth professed her loyalty to the God of Israel and would not return to Moab.

After Naomi and Ruth arrived in Israel, they found themselves destitute. Since Naomi was too old to work, Ruth went out daily to glean the leftover grain in the fields. Through God's providence, Ruth ended up gathering grain in a field owned by Boaz, who graciously looked out for her safety and well-being.

I especially love when Boaz told Ruth, "Have I not commanded the young men not to touch you?"[13] Imagine how frightened Ruth must have been to daily make herself vulnerable by gathering grain in a field where foreign men would likely have not treated her favorably. I get chills when I think about Boaz "riding in on his horse," so to speak, and coming to her rescue. Now, that's a knight-in-shining-armor story! So what made this woman from a foreign land so attractive to Boaz?

In my study Bible[14] I found a list of character qualities that made Ruth not only lovely to look at but inwardly radiant. I believe she personified the traits found in the excellent wife of Proverbs 31. Let's look at those qualities:

Devoted to Her Family

Ruth was *devoted to her family*.[15] She displayed her devotion to her mother-in-law when Naomi entreated her to return to her people. Ruth's response has become a popular quote for couples to cite in one form or another in their wedding ceremonies:

> Entreat me not to leave you, or to turn back from following after you; for wherever you go, I will go; and wherever you lodge, I will lodge; your people shall be my people, and your God, my God. Where you die, I will die, and there will I be buried. The LORD do so to me, and more also, if anything but death parts you and me.[16]

I am moved to tears when I read about how Ruth pledged lifelong devotion to her mother-in-law. Over the years, Steve and I have taught a six-week premarital course and counseled many engaged couples. The most important aspect of this course is helping couples understand that marriage is a covenant, not a contract.

Steve explains, "A contract is something that says, 'If you do this for me, I will do this for you.'" He then goes on to say, "A marriage covenant is an unconditionally binding promise between you and the Lord. You are not making a covenant with your betrothed, but with the Lord."

Do you reflect this kind of devotion to your husband? If Ruth was this committed to her mother-in-law, I can only imagine the loyalty she would have displayed to Boaz when he became her husband. Do you think her devotion would have captured Boaz's attention? I do. And this kind of commitment will certainly capture the affections of your husband as well.

Okay, time-out. Some of you may be saying, "But you don't understand, Rhonda. I am married to a difficult man. Even if I were to be this committed to him, he wouldn't appreciate it. He's a jerk."

Scripture tells us of godly women who were married to jerks. For example, there is the story of Abigail and Nabal, which we find in 1 Samuel 25. Verse 3 says of them, "She was a woman of good understanding and beautiful appearance; but the man was harsh and evil in his doings." Nabal, whose name means "fool," acted terribly toward King David, and Abigail was quick to make amends for what her husband had done.

Somerset County Library System of NJ
Bridgewater branch

Checkouts for WAAG CUR

You can't make me (but I can be persuaded) /
649.64 TOB
33665013282141
Due Date: 12/3/2018

Your money, your marriage : the secrets to sm
332.024 LOW
33665030153804
Due Date: 12/3/2018

The silent sea [a novel of the Oregon files] /
FIC CUSS
33665023353460
Due Date: 12/3/2018

A lifelong love what if marriage is about more
CD 248.844 THOM
33665032809825
Due Date: 12/3/2018

Dealing with the elephant in the room : movinç
153.6 BEC
33665030806401
Due Date: 12/3/2018

The marriage mentor /
248.4 STO
33665032457872
Due Date: 12/3/2018

To renew your materials, visit us online at
SCLSNJ.org, or call 908-458-8408.

11/12/2018 7:32:52 PM

And before the king of Persia took Esther as his queen, he had cruelly humiliated and banished his previous wife for simply not "presenting herself" at a party for all his drunken friends to ogle at (Esther 1:10-12,19).

Esther's grace-filled life left a lasting legacy because her focus was not on the man to whom she was married. Rather, she was devoted to living in obedience to God's plan for her life. If you are married to an unreasonable man, have you considered that God may want to accomplish great feats through you as you keep your sights on Him and determine to grow in the grace and knowledge of our Lord?[17]

Delighted in Her Work

The next character quality that made Ruth beautiful is that she *delighted in her work*.[18] Ruth did not shrink back when the only way she would be able to provide for herself and her mother-in-law was to tie up her skirts and gather grain in the fields. The excellent wife in Proverbs 31 can be found preparing meals, making investments, sewing clothes, and generally doing all those things that we say we want to do but never actually get around to accomplishing. Proverbs 31:27 says the virtuous woman's husband praises her because "she watches over the ways of her household, and does not eat the bread of idleness."

How well do you delight in serving your husband and your family? Are you joyful when you clean the house, pick up the dry-cleaning, or make a meal? Or do you grumble when you have to clean—as though it is some big surprise to you the house got dirty again? Are you constantly so distracted by social media that you neglect your daily tasks? Can your husband and children tell that they are truly the priorities of your life and that you take joy in caring for them?

Dependent upon God

The next shining quality Boaz recognized in Ruth was her dependence on God.[19] Boaz observed it was "the LORD God of Israel, under whose wings [Ruth had] come for refuge" (Ruth 2:12). One great source of security for a godly man is to know his wife is seeking the Lord as she goes about her day. Whether you are working outside the home or managing your household, if your husband knows you are living in full dependence upon God, he can rest assured your choices will be honoring to the Lord. With that assurance, your husband's heart can safely trust you, as did the man married to the Proverbs 31 woman.[20] And when a husband can trust in his wife, adoration is a natural response.

C.H. Spurgeon's father, John, was an extremely busy man. He was often away from home, leaving the task of bringing up the family largely to his wife, Eliza.

One Sunday while on his way to church, John Spurgeon turned the carriage around and returned home out of concern for the spiritual well-being of his children. When he entered the house, he heard the sound of his wife in earnest prayer. C.H. Spurgeon said, "My father felt that he might safely go about his Master's business while his dear wife was caring so well for the spiritual interests of the children."[21]

Would your husband consider you a woman who depends upon God? If he were to come home in the middle of the day, like Spurgeon's father did, would he find you praying for your children or pulling your hair out?

Learning to daily read and apply truth from the Bible and pray throughout your day will help you develop a habit of depending on God. And when you do this...

- Your husband can rest in your godly demeanor.
- Your kids will find security in knowing their mommy regularly seeks wisdom from the Lord.
- Your inner beauty will flourish, and your husband will be attracted to your gentle and quiet spirit, which is precious in God's sight (1 Peter 3:4).

Dedicated to Godly Speech

The next important quality that will make you the apple of your husband's eye is being *dedicated to godly speech*.[22] We are told of the Proverbs 31 woman, "She opens her mouth with wisdom, and on her tongue is the law of kindness" (verse 26).

Do you think before you talk? Or in the heat of the moment, do you just blurt out whatever comes to mind? There is nothing less attractive to a man than a woman with an unbridled tongue, a woman who spouts condescending remarks or venomous slurs.

What are some ways you can be sure you are dedicating yourself to godly speech?

Determine never to make your husband feel inadequate or stupid in public or in private. When he makes a mistake, or shares his thoughts, concerns, or ideas with you, be the one person he can count on to be supportive. When he talks about his ideas, don't make him feel inferior. If you do, he will likely stop sharing his dreams or confiding in you. You don't want that, do you?

Speak kind words. Ephesians 4:32 says, "Be kind one to another." Does your husband cringe when he comes home from work because he wonders whether you are going to meet him with kindness or harshness? Decide today you will only speak kindness to him when he arrives home. If you do, he will likely come to think you are the most beautiful woman on earth. And he will certainly look forward to coming home to see you.

Always speak well of your husband. When your husband is not around, can he trust that what you say about him will be honorable? Do you affirm him in public and speak highly of his accomplishments, or does he worry you might embarrass him by belittling him or revealing one of his secrets?

Your husband wants—in fact, he *needs*—you to be proud of him, and to always have his back. Proverbs 31:12 says an excellent wife "does [her husband] good and not evil all the days of her life."

If you make a constant effort to be your husband's friend and confidant, he will view your worth as being "far above rubies" (Proverbs 31:10) because he will know he can trust you. And a man who treasures his wife will treat her like a treasure.

Practical Ways to Keep His Attention

Along with developing your inner beauty, there are many ways to help your husband have eyes only for you. Here are a few ideas, and I'm sure you can think of more:

1. *Flirt with him.* Catch his eye across a crowded room and give him a flirtatious wink. Whisper in his ear at the dinner table how you plan to enjoy his company later—after the kids are put to bed.

2. *Present yourself so he will be proud of you.* Dress to please him (Proverbs 31:22).

3. *Look joyfully toward the future.* Rejoice in the times to come (Proverbs 31:25).

4. *Forgive him.* And then don't keep a record of his wrongs.[23] In the way you would hope your husband forgets about your past offenses, offer him the same grace.

5. *Have sex with your husband.* Do you realize you are God's gift to him to satisfy his God-given sexual desires? We will discuss this further in chapter 7. But for now—trust me—men whose wives pursue them sexually know they are blessed. Your husband likely knows other men who complain about how disinterested in sex their wives are. If your man is one of the few married men whose wife not only enjoys sex with him but actually pursues him, not only will you keep his attention, but he will slay dragons for you!

From a Husband's Perspective
A Word from Steve

I have raised dogs all of my life. When I was a young man, German shepherds captured my attention. But after a less-than-favorable experience with one of my shepherds, I moved on to golden retrievers. Most retrievers are loyal, friendly, and loving dogs—without the killer instincts of a German shepherd. And as puppies, golden retrievers are generally happy-go-lucky and clueless.

Many of us men may try to come off like the German shepherd, but truth be known, when it comes to knowing how to make our wives feel beautiful or special, many of us are more like clueless puppies.

Through the years, Rhonda has helped me understand how much she needs me to tell her she looks attractive. For me—and many men I have talked to—it is easy to develop an attitude that says, "I told you that you were pretty when I met you. If I change my mind, I'll let you know." But with my wife's sometimes not-so-gentle prompting, it didn't take me long to figure out "That ain't how it's done!"

My beloved has had to remind me numerous times over the years how much she values my words of affirmation. Even after more than 30 years of marriage, she still needs to know I find her attractive. Maybe you can relate.

I'll let you in on a little secret: for some reason I am a little reticent to use the word *pretty* (a confession I have not even shared with Rhonda—until now because she is editing this section for me. Thanks, babe!). My hesitation to use *that* word probably comes from some regressed memory that would take a lot of therapy to get through. However, suffice it to say, *pretty* just doesn't feel like a manly word for me to use. I usually say something like, "Baby, you look hot!" But I digress.

The point is, don't feel hurt if you have to patiently remind your husband of your emotional need to hear him tell you you're attractive to him. We men really want to meet the needs of our wives, but sometimes we feel awkward, or simply forget how much you value our affirmation. If your hubby needs a little prodding, do it patiently and lovingly. Remind him of how much you want to be pretty for him, but tell him you also need to hear from him when you put forth the effort. (If your husband is one who frequently tells you you're beautiful without being reminded, count your blessings and tell him you appreciate his sensitivity.)

While we are on this subject, the next time you ask your husband's opinion about how you look in the outfit you are wearing, don't back him into a corner asking him questions like, "Does my rear look big in these pants?" Seriously—how is a man supposed to answer that question? And if you ask your man to choose between outfit A or outfit B, do him a favor and wear the one he chooses. If you're not willing to do so, you would be wise not to ask his opinion in the first place.

(How would you feel if your husband gave you two options and then promptly dismissed your choice?)

Here is one more insight for you: When Rhonda and I are running late, the last thing I want to tell her is, "Oh, yes, babe, the outfit you had on before looked way better on you. You go ahead and change. I'll just wait in the car and calculate how fast I am going to have to drive to make it to the event on time." Get my point?

The secret to capturing your husband's
attention for a lifetime is in learning to find your
worth in your relationship with Christ.

And remember, rather than focus on developing external beauty that will not stand the test of time, devote yourself to cultivating the beauty that comes from within the heart. As Rhonda pointed out, the secret to capturing your husband's attention for a lifetime is in learning to find your worth in your relationship with Christ. When you spend your life developing your inner beauty and staying focused on the Lord, your husband's affection for you will grow as he observes the lovely woman of God you are becoming. The more consistently you pursue Christ, the more beautiful you will become to your husband, to others, and most importantly, to Christ.

Wives, listen to chapter 6 audio "Finding Your Worth"
RhondaStoppe.com/marriage-mentor

Man to Man

In this chapter Rhonda asked your wives, "Are you a good thing?," a question taken from Proverbs 18:22, "He who finds a wife finds a good thing and obtains favor from the LORD." Rhonda shared with your wife how husbands feel valued not only by a wife who develops her inner beauty but also when she works to look her best for you.

This question may have prompted your wife to do a bit of introspection. And maybe this is a good time to ask of yourself some questions too:

Are *you* a good thing to your wife?

Do you treat her like she is a good thing for you?

Your wife needs to feel valued by you. She wants you to admire her as a person, and she longs to believe you still see her as beautiful. While there are always exceptions, for most women wanting to feel lovely seems to be a part of their nature.

Some would argue that a woman who wants to be affirmed for her external beauty is shallow or even worldly. And yes, many women face problems if they come to think their worth or value is predicated by their looks. I think we can agree our society is full of women who mistakenly measure their worth against the world's definition of beauty (this topic is for a whole different conversation).

But don't questions your wife's spiritual maturity if she needs to hear you compliment her. You and I can learn a thing or two from Song of Solomon's example. This guy was over the top when it came to telling his wife how hot he thought she was. Check this out:

> Behold, you are beautiful, my love;
> Behold, you are beautiful;
> > your eyes are doves…
> Behold, you are beautiful, my love,
> > behold you are beautiful!
> Your eyes are doves
> > behind your veil…
> Your lips are like a scarlet thread,
> > and your mouth is lovely…
> Your two breasts are like two fawns,
> > twins of a gazelle,

that graze among the lilies
(Song of Solomon 1:15; 4:1,3,5 ESV).

When you were dating your wife, did you tell her she was pretty? I'll bet she was drawn to you because of your affirming words. Your wife wants to believe your attraction for her has not grown cold since your days of dating. Complimenting her will help her feel secure in your love for her.

Over the years I've often forgotten to tell Rhonda when I think she looks good. I really do notice when she makes the effort, but I guess when I'm thinking, *Wow! She looks hot*, I somehow believe she can read my mind (which she assures me she cannot).

Now that Rhonda is older, and she's feeling like the years may not have been as kind to her as she would have liked, I'm learning (because she tells me) how much more she needs me to affirm her inner *and* outer beauty. I can either ignore her vulnerable request or I can choose to try harder to say things that will make her feel attractive.

Your wife may not ever ask you to tell her she is pretty, but she is likely hoping you'll remember to do so. I know it's easy to take for granted, but making the effort to tell your wife you are proud to be seen with her and thanking her for taking care of her appearance will encourage your wife and make her secure in your love for her.

From a Wife's Perspective
A Word from Rhonda

Okay, I get it. I'm needy! After I read over Steve's section to husbands, I realized how needy I might sound to you since I ask Steve to tell me I am pretty. Call it what you will, but I look at it more like I'm being honest and vulnerable with him about my need to believe he still finds me attractive after 36 years of marriage.

The way I see it, the Bible calls husbands to live with their wives in an understanding way, but how is my husband ever gonna understand how much I need to hear his affirming words if I don't tell him?

Whether or not your wife asks you, it's my guess that she is hoping you'll notice when she makes an effort to look pretty. And even when she doesn't make the effort—you know, like when she's been up all night with a sick baby and has to roll out of bed early to get the other kids ready for school? She may not look like she's at the top of her game, but on days like that you will encourage her if she thinks you see her beauty shine through as she lovingly cares for your family and forces a tired smile toward you as leave for work.

Beauty is in the eye of the beholder, so be the guy who beholds your wife's inner loveliness and outward splendor. And tell her…yes, tell her, my friend. She needs to hear it.

Together, watch chapter 6 video at
RhondaStoppe.com/marriage-mentor

Thinking It Through

Wives: Explain to your husband how hearing him compliment your beauty makes you feel.

Husbands: Consider the last time you told your wife she is pretty. If you've gotten out of the habit of complimenting your wife, consider making a conscious effort to do so in the future.

Living It Out

Husbands: Think of at least one characteristic about your wife that you find attractive. Maybe it's her smile that you can't wait to see when you walk in the door after a long day at work. Whatever comes to mind, make it a point to tell you wife what you admire and why.

Wives: Remember how important it is to your husband that you present yourself in a manner that he can be proud of. Not just when you're in public, but even at home, make an effort to look pretty for your husband. (Notice I didn't say you have to fit into those skinny jeans that are haunting you from the back of your closet. Rather, do your best to be comfortable in your own skin, and dress in a manner that tells your husband you care about how you look.)

Also, wives, for "extra credit" you can implement this week at least two of the principles you read in the section entitled "The Secret to Keeping His Attention." Observe how your husband responds to your actions.

All He Wants Is Sex

WHEN SHE LONGS FOR ROMANCE

As single adults, Tim and Karen met at church. Karen says, "From the moment he walked in the door, Tim was the guy every single woman had their eye on."

With a twinkle in her eye, Karen told me how delighted she was the first time Tim's gaze met hers across the crowded sanctuary. And with that gaze, Tim became the object of her affection.

Karen said, "Since Tim was a bit awkward in his pursuit, I helped him out by finding reasons to talk to or sit by him at church—you know, to encourage him to pursue me."

Karen smiled as she said, "The day I watched Tim casually saunter across the room to take the seat next to me was the day all the single women knew, 'This guy's off the market.'"

While they were dating, Karen remembers how difficult it had been for them to keep their hands off of each other. To keep their commitment to remain sexually pure until they were married, Tim and Karen determined not to spend time alone. This meant long talks at the coffee shop, walking hand-in-hand at the park, and lots of fun activities.

Karen recalls, "I seriously couldn't wait to give myself to Tim in our marriage bed. And since I was so sexually motivated before marriage, I was convinced I would enjoy sex with my husband."

The honeymoon did not disappoint Tim or Karen, and they thoroughly enjoyed sex for their first two years of marriage. But when Karen took on a job that required her to stand on her feet all day, and Tim's schedule brought him home late in the evening, their sex life took a backseat to everything else.

Karen remembers thinking, *I know we should have sex more often, but I'm just so tired. And Tim doesn't seem to mind—he never says anything anyway.*

As time passed, Tim and Karen found themselves becoming less and less intimate—both in the bedroom and in the way they related to one another. Every night Tim came home and plopped down in front of the television, while Karen busied herself with social media.

What Tim and Karen did not discuss was how unfulfilled and lonely they were feeling in their marriage. Whenever Tim approached Karen for sex, he felt as though she accommodated him out of obligation, not because she wanted him sexually. And since Tim never seemed to pursue her romantically except when he wanted sex, Karen secretly resented Tim's advances.

Does Tim and Karen's story sound familiar? I wish I could say it's not the norm for married Christian couples, but sadly, this scenario is more common than you might think.

When Steve and I were first married, sex was pretty amazing! The Christian books we had read to prepare us for the marriage bed really paid off. Learning one another's bodies was a delightful adventure we both enjoyed.

After a couple of years of marriage, I became pregnant with our first child. I will never forget what a woman at work told me—a woman I didn't know very well. She pulled me aside and said, "Can I give you some advice? When you have your baby, don't make tending to the baby a priority over having sex with your husband. That's a mistake I made when I was a young mom—and it's a mistake you don't want to make."

I remember thinking, *How odd that this older woman would reveal to me such an intimate secret from her past.* But I tucked her words away in the back of my mind.

The first time I heard our baby cry from her room while Steve and I were having sex, the older woman's words of advice rang in my ears.

I knew Meredith was safe in her crib. So I made a decision to *stay in the game*, as it were, and not jump out of bed right that second. We took a moment to finish, then I quickly tended to Meredith. I later learned from my husband how much he appreciated what I had done. My actions told him, "I value you. You are important to me too."

What Does Sex Mean to Him?

Most women understand men have a strong physical desire for sex. So why do wives make their husbands feel apologetic for wanting sex? I think one reason is because a woman's need for sexual intimacy is emotionally driven—we want to feel loved, desired, and beautiful. But when it seems as though a husband's desire for sex is a mere physical urge, it becomes easy to wrongly assume he is acting selfishly and resent it. But what gets overlooked is the fact that a husband's sense of well-being and confidence is very much wrapped up in the sexual intimacy he enjoys with his wife.

Your husband's God-given need to connect
with you physically means just as much to him
as good communication means to you.

For example, as a woman, you likely find great fulfillment in your marriage relationship through conversation. So you might expect your husband to find satisfaction in this as well. But the truth is that while men can enjoy talking with their wives, most men do not find the same fulfillment in conversation as women do. Your husband's God-given need to connect with you physically means just as much to him as good communication means to you.

Neither of you are wrong; you are just wired differently. By design, God made you to feel emotionally connected with your husband through conversation, and He made your husband to emotionally engage with you through sex.

The trouble comes when both husband and wife look past the other person's needs and refuse to give what the other one longs for, in hopes of coercing their spouse to meet their own need. This is always a recipe for disaster.

Make no mistake—refusing to satisfy your husband's deepest need until he gives you the romance you desire will only serve to erode the loving environment you so desperately long for in your marriage.

What do you suppose Jesus would advise wives to do when it comes to ministering to their husband's sexual needs? In Matthew 7:12, Jesus said, "So whatever you wish that others would do to you, do also to them" (esv).

One key way to reflect God's perfect love to others is to treat them the way you want to be treated. In the same way you want your husband to learn how to meet your emotional need for intimacy and romance, God wants you to be willing to understand his emotional need for sex and determine to satisfy his need—whether or not he ever meets yours.

The secret to a happy marriage is to take your eyes off of yourself—and your expectations—and focus on following Christ's example of a humble servant when it comes to loving your husband. Philippians 2:3-8 says:

> Let nothing be done through selfish ambition or conceit, but in lowliness of mind let each esteem others better than himself. Let each of you look out not only for his own interests, but also for the interests of others. Let this mind be in you which was also in Christ Jesus, who, being in the form of God, did not consider it robbery to be equal with God, but made Himself of no reputation, taking the form of a bondservant, and coming in the likeness of men. And being found in appearance as a man, He humbled Himself and became obedient to the point of death, even the death of the cross.

Just as Jesus humbled Himself to serve God by serving others, when you humbly minister to your husband, even in the marriage bed, you are actually serving the Lord.

I Have a Headache

What I see as the primary reason women withhold sex from their husbands is selfishness, plain and simple. "Not tonight—I have a headache" seems to be a common response of wives when a husband shows interest in sex. When you say "not tonight" to your husband, you are rejecting him. He feels the rejection and will respond in a number of ways. Commonly, when husbands feel rejected they'll recoil, or grow agitated or even angry.

"Husbands do not want to beg their wives for sex," said one podcast host I was recently interviewed by. He went on, "If I get shot down too many times, I'll stop asking. Even though I really want to take my wife to bed, the fear of her choosing her pillow over intimacy with me is just something I'm not willing to experience again and again."

Wow, right? How many men feel rejected and misunderstood when their wives, who are super busy doing great things all day long, don't save enough energy to enjoy them sexually.

I know saying it is selfish for a wife to withhold sex may cause the hair on your neck to bristle because the stuff you do all day is likely for everyone else but you. But when you make it a point to prioritize your day so you're not too tired to be with your man, he will see that as a selfless act. Choosing to consider your husband's need for sex over your own desire to get a ton of stuff done by the end of the day is truly selfless. And in the end, when your kids see that your priority is your relationship with their father, you give them a sense of security and well-being that they won't ever realize from your keeping a Pinterest-perfect house—make sense?

Preoccupation with Self

Because of our sin nature, the basic problem all people have is a pre-occupation with self. In short, every sin results from this preoccupation. (Yes, I just implied that not having sex with your husband is a sin that stems from selfishness.)

When you are selfishly devoted to yourself rather than to God and others—in this case, your husband—you will resist giving of yourself to him selflessly. And without Christ's help, you can never reach a standard of selfless love on your own. I mean, let's be honest, it is only through Christ's love that a wife can move toward her husband when resentment or exhaustion might turn her away.

Now, in defense of yourself, you might begin to rattle off a list of "all the things I do for that man." I am sure you are a great wife who does many acts of service for your husband. But allow me to let you in on a little secret my husband shared with me years ago. As a rule, most men would forego a picture-perfect house—or other things—for great sex. Is it possible you may need to rethink your priorities?

If you're feeling a little convicted right now, you may be thinking, *How can I become less self-focused?* Even trying harder not to be self-focused can cause you to remain self-focused. Hebrews 12:2 says we are to be "looking unto Jesus"—that is the only place we should fix our eyes.

Looking back, as a young mother, I remember how my self-focus kept me from ministering to my husband's sexual needs. After a day filled with being climbed upon, nursed on, and touched by my kids, the idea of being touched in bed was something I had trouble wrapping my mind around. Maybe you can relate? But one day this thought occurred to me: *At work Steve is likely using most of the 5000 words an average man speaks in a day, and yet I still expect him to talk to me in the evening. I need to treat him the way I expect to be treated. Even though I have been touched all day, I need to joyfully make myself available to his touch.*

Inspired by this new revelation, I wanted to become a wife who put Steve's needs above my own. And I discovered that the secret to becoming a selfless wife was found in daily Bible study and prayer because time in God's Word transformed me more into the woman God wanted me to be. As a result, my prayers and desires became others-focused rather than all about me. I also found that when I forsook time with the Lord, I became less interested in meeting my husband's needs and more focused on my own.

As you are sanctified by God's truth, repent of your selfishness, and pray for your marriage, the Holy Spirit will enable you to selflessly love your husband. You will want to see your husband's need for sex with Christ's compassion, and even *want* to fulfill his needs — even if your husband isn't making an effort to meet your needs.

One Bible teacher says, "[Selfless love] can only come from the indwelling Holy Spirit, whose first-fruit is love (Gal. 5:22). In Jesus Christ 'the love of God has been poured out within our hearts through the Holy Spirit who was given to us' (Rom. 5:5). Only Christ's own Spirit can empower us to love each other as He loves us (John 13:34)."[1]

He Just Wants You to Want Him

To help you gain insight into how much men want to be wanted by their wives, one survey revealed that 74 percent of men said they would not be satisfied sexually if their wives offered all the sex they wanted but did so reluctantly or simply to accommodate their need.[2]

Shaunti Feldhahn, author of *For Women Only*, shares this insight:

> As much as men want sex, most of them would rather go out and clip the hedges in the freezing rain than make love with a wife who appears to be responding out of duty...If she's just responding because she has to, he's being rejected by his wife...

> Consider the painful words of this truly deprived husband:

> "We've been married for a long time. I deeply regret and resent the lack of intimacy of nearly any kind for the duration of our marriage. I feel rejected, ineligible, insignificant, lonely, isolated and abandoned as a result. Not having the interaction I anticipated prior to marriage is like a treasure lost and irretrievable. It causes deep resentment and hurt within me. This in turn fosters anger and feelings of alienation."[3]

When you mistakenly view your husband's need for sex as some sort of primal urge to be satisfied from time to time, you are missing the true ministry God has given you to affirm your husband's deepest emotional needs through sex.

Did you know that when you pursue your husband sexually, you have a profound influence on him in all areas of his life? Men tend to struggle with feelings of inadequacy and loneliness. When you find your husband sexually desirable, and he feels loved for who he is, then you fill him with a sense of strength, well-being, and confidence.

Men are more confident and alive when they are enjoying a healthy sex life with their wives. "One husband said, 'What happens in the bedroom really does affect how I feel the next day at the office.' Another wrote, 'Sex is a release of day-to-day pressures…and seems to make everything else better.'"[4]

When your husband says he feels better after you have sex with him, you would be wise to understand he is *not* simply talking about the physical pleasure he experiences through lovemaking. He may never be able to put into words the effect making love to you has on his emotional well-being. But it really does impact him in a big way. You just watch and see if the results aren't reflected in your husband's confidence and overall satisfaction with life.

But I Want Romance!

When Steve and I were dating, he would drive 30 minutes across town during his lunch break just to drop off a bouquet of flowers. Because he had to get back to work before his lunch hour was over, he only had time to knock on the door, hand me the flowers, give me a kiss, and then jump back in his car.

As I watched Steve drive away, I would bury my face in the flowers and say, "Oh, how romantic!"

After we were married, Steve often stopped by the flower shop on his way home from work to bring me lovely bouquets. When I became a stay-at-home mom, Steve continued the romantic practice of bringing me flowers. Only this time I did not say, "Oh, how romantic!" Rather, I said, "Oh, how expensive!"

I made a big mistake when I said that. When my husband's romantic gesture was met with my practical "this doesn't fit our stay-at-home-mom" budget, I did not realize how my words discouraged him. He was attempting to keep the romance alive in our marriage by doing the one thing I had told him was romantic since our days of courtship. In one fell swoop I had made him feel like he had failed in his attempt to be romantic *and* made him feel bad we were on a tight budget.

Don't mistakenly assume husbands don't care about making romantic gestures. A 2004 survey showed that 84 percent of men say they do want to be romantic,[5] but most say they just don't know what romance looks like to their wives. So help your husband understand what is romantic to you.

Steve and I had a discussion about romance before I sat down to write this chapter. He explained, "We men really do want to be romantic, but for most of us this means getting out of our comfort zone. When we are afraid we won't measure up to our wife's expectations, it's tempting to just not try at all."

Steve went on, "I know that giving gifts is romantic, but I always put so much pressure on myself to think of romantic gifts to the point I end up at a loss."

I then pointed out to Steve how I found it very romantic when he builds something for me. For example, I recently asked him to make a wardrobe mirror for me. He was not sure he agreed with my request to build the mirror's frame out of the reclaimed barn wood we had on our property, but he complied.

Within a few days, I had the most amazing wardrobe mirror, framed with shabby-chic barn wood, leaning up against the wall in my bedroom. I *loved* it! So much so I posted a picture of the mirror on Instagram. (Follow me @RhondaStoppe to see more #StoppeEverAfter posts.) This one post created a great deal of chatter among my Instagram followers about how much they wanted my husband to make a mirror for them as well. To which I replied, "He just does this for me." To me *that's* romance!

So what says *romance* to you? You cannot very well expect your husband to know if you're not even sure of the answer yourself. So take some time to consider some of your husband's romantic gestures in the past. And then tell him how you found those actions romantic. For example, when our children were young, I made sure Steve knew the most romantic thing he could do for me was to clean up the dinner dishes and get the kids bathed and into bed—while I took a hot bath. This romantic act was most certainly met with a grateful wife and some sweet lovemaking that evening.

When your husband makes an effort to be romantic, help him know when he is on the right track. Remember, he is likely putting himself in a situation where he feels inadequate. This means your husband might think he is risking humiliation if he gets it wrong. He may even believe he will lose your respect if his attempt at romance fails. So if he ruins the dinner he was making or—as in my case—he pays too much for flowers you can't afford, don't humiliate him.

One man said, "If I make the effort to be romantic and she laughs at me, you can be sure I won't put myself in that vulnerable position again for a very long time."

How Does Your Husband Define Romance?

Hopefully this chapter is helping you understand that when your husband desires sex, he is not simply looking for a physical release. He likely longs for romance as well. So if most men truly are closet romantics, let's look at what speaks *romance* to your man.

Remember when you were dating? How did you spend your time together as a couple? Did your husband sit across from you reading poetry or singing songs he wrote just for you as he gazed into your eyes? Probably not. (Or maybe he did, if you're married to an artsy kind of guy.) At any rate, I imagine your courtship hours were spent talking and playing together as a couple.

If you are like most women, the talking and listening you experienced from your husband-to-be filled your romance tank. By contrast, the times of playing together would likely have ranked number one on your husband's romance chart.

Which brings me to the first activity most men find romantic: *Play with your husband.* What does he like to do? What activities did you enjoy doing together when you were dating? Did you hike, play golf, or go fishing? If joining your husband in such activities filled up your husband's romance tank then, most likely it will do the same today. (As long as you go along to enjoy his company, and not to invade his solitude with nagging or complaints about everyday-life issues he may be trying to escape through his playtime.)

The Day I Became a Biker Chick

The year our oldest daughter, Meredith, turned 18, my husband came home with a motorcycle. He wanted me to ride on the back with him while leaving our two younger kids at home with Meredith. Up to this point, I had been hesitant to ride with Steve. I thought, *Who will take care of our kids if something happens to us?*

But now that Meredith was 18, Steve thought it was a great time to buy a motorcycle. His logic was, "If something happens to us, Meredith can take care of the kids."

Seriously, Steve thought this made perfect sense. So I had a choice to make: I could succumb to my fear, or I could jump on the back of that bike, wrap my arms around my man, and ride off into the sunset.

I chose the latter.

And over the past decade, what adventures we have had on our motorcycle! Recently we rode the bike from northern California to Seattle and back—1,900 miles round trip! This experience was pure romance for my husband. And I completely enjoyed the scenery as we rode the coastal highway. As for my romantic tank? Once we made it to Seattle, we caught a cruise ship to Alaska and had a delightful time of romance!

Just like you enjoy time with your girlfriends, there are times your husband would prefer to do activities with his guy friends. But you may be surprised to learn that your husband might not always be looking for guys to do guy stuff with him. Rather, he might be hoping *you* will do guy stuff with him. And when you do, he is romanced.

Here are two more activities that may fill your husband's need for romance:

Let him pursue you. When you were dating your husband, part of the romance for him was in pursuing you. So devise ways to flirt with and entice him into pursuing you from time to time. When it comes to filling your husband's need for romance, you'll be surprised how far a little flirtation goes.

Have sex with him. When your husband puts forth the effort to pursue you, he is really hoping the evening will end with him enjoying you sexually. And as we discussed earlier, his desire is for you to be looking forward to your time together as well.

When you joyfully take your husband to bed, you not only satisfy his physical, God-given need for sex, you become the salve for his soul as well. When you make the effort to deeply engage with your husband through sex, you are saying to him, "I love you. I want you. I am here for you. I believe in you." Is it any wonder why most men put sex as number one in their romance category?

Secrets of Great Sex

What if you don't enjoy sex? You're not the only woman who has wondered about this. While this book is not about how to have great sex, I have written an ebook titled *A Christian Woman's Guide to Great Sex in Marriage.* (To obtain a copy visit NoRegretsWoman.com.)

I will let you in on a little secret: the longer you take to enjoy foreplay in the marriage bed, the more your body will prepare you for an incredible sexual experience. While amidst the busyness of life "quickies" are an important way to connect with your husband sexually, do make time for some marathon sex once in a while.

As women, when we go without sexual satisfaction for a period of time, we tend to forget how much we like it, while the opposite is true of men. So taking the time to create great sexual encounters will make you want more of those experiences in the future. (And if you have trouble reaching orgasm through intercourse, know that around 75 percent of women have the same challenge. Read my ebook for insights about this issue.)

If you don't enjoy sex, perhaps it's because you had a bad sexual experience in the past. In my case, I was molested when I was six years old. So early in our marriage, I had to learn how not to flashback to that experience while Steve and I were making love. By forgiving the man who violated me, talking to my husband about my struggle, and prayer together as a couple and in my own personal prayers—often in the moment I was having the flashback—I was able to conquer the destructive emotions and enjoy sex with my husband.

If you have been violated, or perhaps you feel shame over sexual encounters you had before marriage, you may want to seek out professional help from a biblical counselor.[6]

Satan loves secrets because they allow him to keep his grip on you. For me, my own abuse as a child played itself out in my early teens through inappropriate physical involvement with boys. It took me more than a decade to even say out loud what I had experienced as a child—or realize how that experience had affected me. But when I made the effort to get godly counsel, my openness took away the shame and fear I had harbored for so many years.

God delights in your marriage bed, and through godly counsel, you can be free of anything that would steal, kill, or destroy the good God planned for sex between you and your man.

So What's the Bottom Line?

Great sex doesn't happen by accident. Life is busy, so having sex with your husband can easily become a less-than-pressing issue for you. Yet it is critical to the health of your marriage that you schedule times in your week for sex—and romance as well.

When you romance your husband, cultivate passionate sexual experiences, and help your husband know how to fill up your romance tank, you will not only transform your sex life, but I believe your marriage will be fundamentally changed as well. You hold the key to building a romantic marriage. By applying the principles in this chapter, you can enjoy a passionate marriage that is deeply satisfying for both of you.

From a Husband's Perspective
A Word from Steve

Rhonda pretty much hit this spot-on regarding the frustration we men have in the romance department. Truth be known, I wasn't really that good at romance before we were married. When we were courting, Rhonda was just keen to look for, and encourage me, when I was being romantic. Did you do this for your husband too? What if, as you did when you were dating your husband, you were to continue to watch for—and celebrate—even his simplest attempts to be romantic? If you do, you may find your husband trying harder to be romantic with you.

So what about sex? At the risk of being categorized as the guy who just wants sex from his wife "because men are animals," I'll roll up my sleeves and try my best to tackle the topic of what sex means to a man. I feel like I am stepping out on a tightrope, but here goes...

When a husband knows his wife desires him sexually, it gives him a special sense of empowerment. This feeling of empowerment, however, is not about "conquering his woman," nor is it arrogance. Rather, it is a quiet confidence that comes over a man when he believes his wife actually wants to make love to him.

I realize that for Christians, our confidence comes from Christ alone. But God also made men to need affirmation in the marriage bed. Have you considered how the Spirit may use you to bolster your husband's self-assurance? When you minister to your husband's deep need for sexual intimacy, you pour courage into his heart.

In this chapter, Rhonda addressed the sin of selfishness and how it enters this whole equation of intimacy. Let's look at what Philippians 2:3-4 (ESV) says: "Count others more significant than yourselves. Let each of you look not only to his own interests, but also to the interests of others."

If God wants you to put the needs of others before your own—with regard to every person you encounter—how much more important is this attitude in the most intimate relationship you can have this side of glory?

When my wife puts my needs above her own through intimacy, she helps me keep my focus on my Savior. She inspires me to continue in my labor of serving Him and brings a sense of fulfillment in the life God has given me.

Rhonda's selflessness empowers me to be effective for God's kingdom. And you may be delighted to find your husband energized to accomplish whatever God is calling him to do as well. In my experience, husbands who are sexually satisfied at home are deeply in love with their wives. I wholeheartedly agree with Rhonda's statement that "when you find your husband sexually desirable, and he feels loved for who he is, then you fill him with a sense of strength, well-being, and confidence." And since selflessly having sex with your husband is truly serving Christ, you will be rewarded by our loving Savior as well!

Wives, listen to chapter 7 audio "What Sex Means to Him" at **RhondaStoppe.com/marriage-mentor**

Man to Man

If you've been married for any length of time, you've likely come to realize that there is a big difference in the way you and your wife view intimacy. I find it interesting that God specifically made us to be different. And contrary to what you might think, our differences are not a result of mankind's sin. By God's design the differences in you and your wife actually work together to create unity in your marriage relationship—if you understand and value the differences.

God's Gift

God gave to married couples the gift of sexual intimacy to be enjoyed under His approving and gracious hand. Have you ever thought about that? Hebrews 13:4 reveals God's perspective on marriage: "Marriage is honorable among all, and the bed undefiled." That means God doesn't just "tolerate" our need for sex; He actually considers it honorable. What a great scripture. Isn't it freeing to know God is interested in you and your wife enjoying great sex in marriage?

Sadly, sin has distorted and perverted God's beautiful gift of sexual intimacy. Sex seems to have become the driving force in our culture and is viewed as nothing more than a human biological function that we cannot help but enjoy.

From ad campaigns to magazines and movies, sexual perversion has pretty much influenced every area of our world, our culture, and our lives. Humanistic thinking has distorted true intimacy by leading people to believe that intercourse is the most important piece to the human relationship between a man and a woman.

All He Wants Is Sex!

As a pastor I have heard women complain, "All he ever wants is sex." And I have heard men say, "She never, ever wants sex." So how can a husband and wife come together to enjoy sex *and* romance in marriage?

Since in this chapter your wife heard what sex means to you, it is only fair to help you learn what romance means to her. Now, I want you to keep an open mind. If your wife habitually withholds sex from you, try to believe the best about her and take an honest evaluation of your circumstance. Ask yourself:

- Is it possible she doesn't want intimacy because she feels like sex with you has become more of a one-sided routine — a duty?

- Is it possible making love to you is a chore for her because you have stopped trying to romance her?

- Do you take time to make the sexual experience good for your wife before you look for your own needs to be met?

In case you're wondering, I'm willing to bet your wife really does want romance; most women do. It's your job to figure out what *she* thinks is romantic. Rhonda has encouraged your wife to be sensitive to your needs, and she tried to explain what that looks like in this chapter. I would say to you it's time you make the effort to understand your wife's desires as well. If you are not sure, ask her what would please her both in the marriage bed and leading up to intimacy.

Remember, in your marriage vows you promised to serve your wife. I am sure you realize that promise goes far beyond the bedroom. You would be wise to know your wife well and be sensitive to listen to her express her needs and desires.

Putting your wife's need for romance above
your own need for sex brings glory to God.

Putting your wife's need for romance above your own need for sex brings glory to God. I cannot give you an ironclad guarantee how you serving your wife will affect your love life, but it couldn't hurt to try, right? As a result, two things might happen: First, it may increase the number of times you have sex each week, while making sex more fulfilling for both of you. And second, you will be honoring your Savior by being obedient to live with your wife according to your knowledge, and by fulfilling your promise to love and serve her faithfully.

From a Woman's Perspective
A Word from Rhonda

Most marriages go through seasons where sex falls low on the list of priorities, especially when raising little ones. Moms are usually exhausted from sleepless nights with a crying baby or from running all day to keep up with a toddler. By the time her head hits the pillow, most women in this season would agree all they can think about is sleep. So throw the poor girl a lifeline, and rather than adding intimacy to your wife's to-do list, give her a back rub. And maybe try to lift some of her burdens so she can have a few minutes to herself before it's time for bed.

If your wife is a mother, she's likely had her "momma hat" on all day long. It's sometimes hard for women to change gears. After seeing herself as the nurturer-mother all day long, it can be difficult to wrap her head around seeing herself as your lover. I often say, "We women have had our 'momma hat' on all day long. A wise husband will take over with the kids and allow their wife to go find her 'sexy momma hat.' It's likely somewhere under the bed collecting dust bunnies, but if you give your wife a few minutes alone in the shower, she just might pull out that 'sexy momma hat' to enjoy a memorable evening with you."

For wives, romance begins way before their husband takes them to bed. As much as you want your wife to give herself to you intimately, realize how much she wants you to give yourself to her through conversation and loving gestures. Try texting her loving words throughout the day or helping her with the dinner dishes and just see if that doesn't light her fire later that night.

Together, watch chapter 7 video at
RhondaStoppe.com/marriage-mentor

Thinking It Through

Read Philippians 2:1-16, and answer the following questions:

1. From verses 2-4, list the instructions Paul gives to Christ's followers.

2. How can you apply the truth of verses 3-4 to your marriage? More specifically, how should you apply this instruction to your sex life?

3. According to verse 5, believers are supposed to "have this mind among yourselves, which is yours in Christ Jesus"

(ESV). What is one Christlike quality you should apply to the way you think toward your spouse and their specific needs for intimacy?

4. Discuss insights you learned regarding the emotional benefits a healthy sex life has on your marriage.

So neither of you are too tired or too disconnected to want to enjoy sexual intimacy with each other, think about ways you can connect with each other throughout the day to lead up to an enjoyable evening together.

Living It Out

Discuss some of the things that interfere with your making time for intimacy. Wives, honestly share any possible reasons why you may be shying away from lovemaking and be willing to offer your husband real insights into how he can romance you in a way that will draw you toward making time for intimacy with him.

List some practical steps each of you will take to make lovemaking more satisfying and more of a priority in your marriage. Talk about how you will work together to implement those steps. And if there are deep-rooted reasons why you have an aversion to sex with your spouse, please seek out a professional who can help you unpack the reasons for your trouble and help you take steps toward enjoying sex freely within the bonds of matrimony.

Every Couple Fights

EIGHT STEPS TO MAKING PEACE

When Julie and Greg were married, neither of them anticipated the baggage Julie was bringing into their relationship from her first marriage. Julie Gorman, author of *What I Wish My Mother Had Told Me About Men*, says, "In an attempt to keep from being hurt, I added more and more conditions to my growing list of needs…Our marriage continued to weaken. Though we loved each other passionately, we also fought passionately. As our fights progressed, our Christian conduct regressed. Expletive adjectives assailed our once-redeemed vocabulary. Four-letter words became a common exchange…I was desperate, needy, and extremely smothering. His growing hostility culminated into an eruption.

"That's when it happened: the frightful night of painful revelation… the night that demanded my change…the night God got hold of my attention in order to set me free."[1]

It wasn't until Greg stormed out of the house shouting, "I love you, Julie—but I can't live like this any longer!" that Julie realized the fragile state of her marriage. And only then did Julie fall to the floor and cry out to God for His help.

And God did help. Julie says, "I'd love to say God healed our marriage instantaneously, but He didn't…it took at least a year for the Holy

Spirit to overhaul our relationship and realign our thoughts with His. But that night…that fight…changed everything…And it provided a foundation that would heal our marriage."[2]

Looking back, Julie says, "I was a control freak! I had constantly tried to align Greg to my endless conditions. I wanted—no, needed—him to function within my controlled environment. Any deviation threatened my security."[3]

So Why Do You Fight?

Fortunately for Greg and Julie, their story ends happily. But after more than 30 years of mentoring women, I am sad to say I have seen too many couples run to divorce court when the "final fight" erupts between them.

Whenever you and your husband have a disagreement, does it turn into a battle? Or maybe you're not a couple who resorts to name-calling or four-letter words, but what about the silent treatment? Couples who don't learn how to resolve conflict in a Christ-honoring way will tend to either lash out with angry words or—just as harmful—ignore one another. Both kinds of responses hurt the relationship.

So why would two people who promised to love one another till their dying breath resort to fighting with one another whenever a disagreement surfaces? James 4:1-2 offers this insight: "What causes quarrels and what causes fights among you? Is it not this, that your passions are at war within you? You desire and do not have, so you murder. You covet and cannot obtain, so you fight and quarrel" (ESV).

James is saying that, ultimately, selfish desires are the cause of quarrels. And because one or both people in the conflict are focused on what they wrongly believe they *must* have to be happy, they will "fight to the death" to get what they want. And for some, this means the death of their marriage. Do you feel so strongly about getting your way that you will fight for it?

Years ago, Steve and I were counseling a married couple who was constantly fighting. On more than one occasion, the police had been called to subdue the husband after he became extremely angry.

When the husband visited alone with Steve, he said, "I don't know why I get so angry. She just talks so fast and comes at me with so many accusations. Before I can respond to one, she is on to the next." Finally, out of frustration of not being able to get a word in edgewise, this husband had put his fist through the wall.

At the same time, when I met privately with the wife, she went through a long list of ways her husband had let her down. She shared with me that each time she began to tell her husband what he had done *once again* not to measure up to her expectations, his defenses went up, her voice got more shrill, and the two would jump headlong into another battle.

It was easy for Steve and me to see how both contributed to their volatile arguments, but since each was convinced they alone were right—and their spouse was wrong—they would not change the way they related to one another in times of conflict. Sadly, their hurtful words and destructive actions chipped away at their marriage until it was destroyed.

But How Do We Stop the Fighting?

If you and your husband have developed a habit of fighting with each other or torturing one another with the silent treatment, know that bad habits do not end by merely *wanting* to stop them. As with anything in life, success comes from hard work. And that is true about healthy conflict resolution.

It is not enough to merely read the Bible and pray for a marriage free from conflict. Along with prayer, you must study the Scriptures and yield in obedience to what you learn. Listen to how desperately the psalmist yearned to keep God's statutes:

> Oh, that my ways were directed to keep Your statutes! Then I would not be ashamed, when I look into all Your commandments...Your word I have hidden in my heart, that I might not sin against You...I have rejoiced in the way of Your testimonies, as much as in all riches. I will meditate on Your precepts, and contemplate Your ways. I will delight myself in your statutes; I will not forget Your word (Psalm 119:5-6,11,14-16).

The key to change is for you to determine that obeying God's
precepts is more important than having your own way.

Are you truly desperate to keep God's statutes? If there is discord in
your marriage, the key to change is for you to determine that obeying
God's precepts is more important than having your own way.

"But how do I apply Scripture to my life?" you ask. In his book *The
Pursuit of Holiness*, Jerry Bridges offers these practical steps: "As you
read or study the Scriptures and then mediate on them during the day,
ask yourself these three questions:

- What does this passage teach concerning God's will for
  a holy life?

- How does my life measure up to that Scripture?…
  Be specific; don't generalize.

- What definite steps of action do I need to take to obey?"

Bridges goes on to say, "Avoid general commitments to obedience
and instead aim for specific obedience…We deceive ourselves when
we grow in knowledge of the truth without specifically responding to
it (James 1:22)."[4]

While it is glorious to delight in what Jesus did on the cross to save
you, rejoicing in the gospel coupled with repentance and yielding yourself in obedience to God's Word is what will transform you into a wife
who can resist the temptation to fight with your husband.

As you wrestle with old habits, don't get discouraged if you don't
find instant victory. Any training requires hard work, and you can
expect that at first you will experience some failures. But if you persevere in this process of studying what God's Word says about your
sin and prayerfully apply it to your life, you will gradually see progress. Eventually you will succeed more often than you fail, until one
day heated conflicts with your spouse become a distant memory. And
when your passion for Christ overrides your passion to win an argument, you'll enjoy peace in your marriage relationship.

So the next time you look longingly at a genuinely happy couple and say, "I bet they never fight. I wish our marriage was as happy as theirs," realize they didn't just *get* a happy marriage and you *got* a difficult one. No, you can be sure a happily married couple makes a determined effort to be happy and to resolve their conflicts in a way that does not tear down their marriage.

Eight Steps to Making Peace

Once you decide to apply biblical principles to how you handle conflict in your marriage, you will bring peace into your home. Here are eight practical steps to beginning the process:

1. Admit You Have a Problem

Stop saying, "I'm fine" or "Everything is fine" when it isn't. For example, if you and your husband have occasional fights that result in hurtful words or actions, *you have a problem*. Or if your disagreements result in days or even weeks of the two of you not speaking to one another, *you have a problem*. And if your husband says whatever he thinks you want to hear to keep the peace, *you have a problem*.

Maybe most of your fights occur at a certain time of the month, and when your hormones settle down, you tell yourself, "The fight wasn't all that bad. He knows I didn't mean what I said. It was just my hormones. He just needs to understand I can't help myself." If so, *you have a problem!*

After you admit you have a problem, the next step to peace is…

2. Acknowledge Your Sinful Bent

We are all fallen creatures who are susceptible to sin. And in Genesis 3:16, God told Eve the consequences that all women would experience as a result of her disobedience: "To the woman He said, 'I will greatly multiply your pain in childbirth; in pain you will bring forth children; yet your desire will be for your husband, and he will rule over you'" (NASB).

Ever since Adam and Eve sinned in the garden, marriage has been plagued by two people who are bent on getting their own way. One Bible teacher observes,

> Because of sin…husbands and wives will face struggles in
> their own relationship. Sin has turned the harmonious sys-
> tem of God-ordained roles into distasteful struggles of self-
> will…Husbands and wives will need God's help in getting
> along as a result. The woman's desire will be to lord it over
> her husband, but the husband will rule by divine design
> (Ephesians 5:22-25).[5]

At the onset of a disagreement, are you willing to ask yourself if your
bent toward trying to rule over your husband is at the root of the conflict? Will you then yield your self-will to God's plan for marriage and
ask Him to help you submit to the authority *He* has placed over you?
Even if your husband is not acting in a respectful manner, out of obedience to God's command you are to offer respect to your husband. One
way to do this, for example, is to respond softly when your husband is
harsh. Proverbs 15:1 says, "A soft answer turns away wrath, but a harsh
word stirs up anger" (ESV).

In Genesis 3:16, when God promised women would have pain in
childbirth, He wasn't kidding. With my first baby, I endured 52 hours
of labor—without any pain meds! So we all agree having a baby hurts.

Along with the pain in childbirth, women are plagued with
monthly periods, cramps, and hormone issues. Let's visit the topic
of hormones, shall we? After my third child was born, I was left with
postpartum depression. And later I was plagued with terrible PMS.
So when my hormone levels dropped, I became weepy and agitated. I
experienced horrible feelings of being out of control, along with bouts
of anxiety.

One day when I was crying—ranting, really—to Steve about how
hard my life was, I looked into his face and saw him trying desperately to understand how he could make things better for me. In that
moment, the Lord opened my eyes to see how much I was hurting my
husband—and our marriage. I decided right then I would never again
allow myself to vent my frustrations to him while my hormones were
affecting me. After that, for a few days each month I withdrew from my
husband and kids to keep from treating them harshly. This also proved

to be hurtful to my husband because my actions made him feel like I was rejecting him or giving him the silent treatment.

When I tried to explain to Steve how hormonal changes in my body influenced the way I interacted with him and the kids, he just looked hurt and disappointed. Finally, I figured out an analogy I could use to help Steve grasp my situation. I said, "Imagine if every time there's a full moon, you turn into a werewolf—no matter how hard you try not to. So your only hope is to ask the people you dearly love to lock you up, and keep you locked up, until the full moon has passed so you don't attack or hurt anyone. *That's* what PMS is like for me. I can't stop it, I know it's coming, and the best thing I can hope for is to keep away from those I love until I am myself again."

I wish you could have seen Steve's face. The werewolf analogy not only gave him a glimpse of the lack of control I feel when my hormones act up, but it also gave him a sense of how he could best help me get through such times—by keeping the kids occupied and giving me as much space as possible for those few days.

Because I was willing to admit *I have a problem*—rather than blaming Steve for the way I was acting—I helped my husband see how desperately I needed his help and understanding.[6] (And now, as a middle-aged woman, I am having to ask Steve once again to understand not only the emotions that go along with menopause but also the crazy hot flashes!)

Once you have admitted you have a problem and have acknowledged you have a sinful bent to be reckoned with, the next step to keeping peace in your relationship is…

3. Refuse to Be Argumentative

Have you ever been with a couple, and no matter what the husband says, the wife is ready to correct him? While the couple bickers back and forth, I find myself thinking, *Who cares if the story your husband is telling happened on Tuesday or Wednesday? And why do you think we want to hear you argue with your husband about who said what to whom and when?*

I don't know about you, but for me to spend an evening with a couple who quarrels is an exhausting experience. I cannot imagine how worn out a person would feel if they lived in a constant state of conflict. Listen to what Proverbs 27:15-16 says about a quarrelsome wife: "A continual dripping on a very rainy day and a contentious woman are alike; whoever restrains her restrains the wind, and grasps oil with his right hand."

And consider these instructions from the apostle Paul: "The Lord's servant must not be quarrelsome but kind to everyone, able to teach, patiently enduring evil...eager to maintain the unity of the Spirit in the bond of peace...If possible, so far as it depends on you, live peaceably with all" (2 Timothy 2:24; Ephesians 4:3; Romans 12:18 ESV).

Because conflict steals our joy, causes anxiety, and robs us of our peace, immediately after Paul addressed the two women who were in conflict at the church in Philippi he said,

> Rejoice in the Lord always; again I will say, rejoice. Let your reasonableness be known to everyone. The Lord is at hand; do not be anxious about anything, but in everything by prayer and supplication with thanksgiving let your requests be made known to God. And the peace of God, which surpasses all understanding, will guard your hearts and your minds in Christ Jesus.[7]

The next time you feel like arguing with your husband, remember 1 Corinthians 13:4-5: love does not insist on having its own way, nor is it irritable or resentful. By refusing to be argumentative, you will show Christ's love to your husband and initiate peace in your relationship. Which leads me to the next step to establishing peace in your relationship:

4. Make Peace a Priority

Get rid of whatever causes discord in your marriage. Whether you and your husband fight over finances, how to spend your free time, or how to discipline your children, it's time to STOP! No argument is worth winning when the love and unity of your marriage is at stake.

I have heard couples bicker and get into full-blown arguments over the most insignificant issues—all because they want what they want. Because of the stress involved in preparing for and going on a vacation, that's when some couples get into their biggest arguments. Others argue each month over their lack of money to cover their bills. If you are fighting over where or how to take a trip, don't take the trip. And if you have a monthly battle over not having enough money, look at how you can downsize or sell what you don't need. And then realize that ultimately, God is your provider, not your husband.

I remember one couple who came to Steve and me for advice. They were so strapped financially that both husband and wife had to work long hours each week to pay their bills, which meant their three teenagers were left unsupervised at home late into the evenings. After the wife shared about their financial burdens, the lack of intimacy in their marriage, and concern over their children, I gently suggested they consider selling some of their possessions and moving into a house they could more readily afford. That would then allow them to cut back on the number of hours they had to work.

In response, the woman explained how inconvenient it would be to move, how uncomfortable they would be in a smaller house, and how she worked hard to have nice things. Therefore, she was unwilling to make any changes. I said, "If my children were at risk and my marriage was in trouble, I would sell all I had, move into an apartment, and work to bring healing to my family."

Sadly, she did not like my response. Within a year, she and her husband were divorced. They moved into separate apartments, and the kids ended up being less supervised than before.

King Solomon, the wisest man who ever lived, said, "Better is a dinner of herbs where love is than a fattened ox and hatred with it."[8] I agree with Solomon—it's better to enjoy love and live on salad every night than to have prime rib all the time and be in a hateful marriage. I'll take lettuce and love over steak and snarls any day—how about you?

Now, you may be thinking, *I hear what you are saying, Rhonda, but I am not the one who is argumentative. My husband picks at everything I do and is constantly looking for a fight.* If this is your situation, my heart goes out to you. I can only imagine how discouraged you may feel. And while I cannot change your husband, I know who can—God.

I have a dear friend whose harsh husband became more peaceable when she stopped fighting with him and trusted God to change him. And God can work wonders through your obedience as well.

When you determine to practice righteous living no matter how your husband responds, God can bring His peace into your relationship. "Peace cannot be divorced from holiness. 'Righteousness and peace have kissed each other' is the beautiful expression of Psalm 85:10. Where there is true peace, there is righteousness, holiness, and purity. May those things characterize you as you strive to be a peacemaker."[9]

So what can you do as you wait on God to change your husband? In these final steps to making peace, here are a few suggestions from God's Word:

5. Pray Without Ceasing

It is the effectual, fervent prayer of the righteous that avails much, so keep your heart pure before the Lord, and never stop praying for God to help your husband grow to be more like Christ (see 1 Thessalonians 5:17; James 5:16; 1 Peter 3:12). And if your husband is not a Christian, never give up praying for his salvation.

6. Forgive Your Husband as Many Times as Necessary

Don't keep a list of your husband's infractions to throw in his face the next time he lets you down. In Matthew 18:22, Jesus instructed us to forgive 70 times 7. His point? Be willing to forgive—always. While our natural fleshly tendency toward withholding forgiveness makes this very difficult to do, remember that through Christ's strength, all things are possible (see Philippians 4:13; Matthew 19:26).

7. Seek Godly Counselors

Look for an older Christian woman whom you trust, and ask her to pray with you and teach you from the Bible how to love your husband. Read Christian books about marriage. And consider seeking advice from your pastor or a biblical counselor[10] (see Titus 2:1-5).

8. Learn to Be a Peacemaker

Jesus said, "Blessed are the peacemakers."[11] You can trust that God will bless you when you determine to be a wife who makes peace with her husband.

What Is a Peacemaker and How Can I Become One?

As a middle child, I have many memories of being curled up on the couch with my fingers in my ears as I watched my siblings fight with one another. Because of this experience, I learned to shut down — or flee — whenever I was exposed to conflict. Since I would avoid conflict at all costs, I considered myself a *peacekeeper*. But I later learned that being a peacekeeper and a peacemaker are not the same thing.

In his book *The Peacemaker*, author Ken Sande says,

> Peacemakers are people who breathe grace. They draw continually on the goodness and power of Jesus Christ, and then they bring His love, mercy, forgiveness, strength, and wisdom to the conflicts of daily life. God delights to breathe His grace through peacemakers and use them to dissipate anger, improve understanding, promote justice, and encourage repentance and reconciliation...I have observed how even the most difficult...issues can be resolved constructively when even one...decides to breathe grace in the midst of conflict.[12]

When people are faced with conflict, they will usually respond in one of two ways:

- Flee from the conflict
- Attack the one with whom they are in conflict

When you find yourself in conflict, which response is your natural tendency? The kind of family you grew up in may have a lot to do with how you respond when conflict arises. For example, if you come from a family where parents and siblings exhibited the attack response, you may have learned the same behavior. Or if you came from a family who "stuffed" their feelings to escape conflict, you may turn and run whenever an argument begins.

Can you imagine how troubling it would be for a person who chooses to *flee* to have their spouse continue to *attack* them verbally while the person tries to avoid the conflict? The one in flight may be thinking, *I would have to really despise someone to treat them like this. They must really hate me to say such hurtful things.* (Take it from a person who flees—whenever someone comes at me aggressively with hateful words, I instinctively think, *They must hate me!*)

At the same time, the spouse who is in attack mode may feel like the one who is trying to escape doesn't care enough to fight it out. Do you see how either response—*flee* or *attack*—can serve to undermine and eventually destroy harmony in a marriage?

Biblical Conflict Resolution

The only way to build a marriage free of hurtful conflict is through biblical conflict resolution. Are you ready to roll up your sleeves and do the hard work of learning the right way to resolve conflict in your marriage? Here are some steps you can take to work through disputes with your spouse in a Christlike manner:

Ask God to help you bring glory to Him by how you respond to conflict. When two imperfect people live together, there is bound to be conflict. A good marriage is defined by how you and your husband respond when you have disagreements.

Looking for ways to reflect Christ's love to your husband when you see the beginning of a dispute will do more to strengthen your relationship with your husband than you can imagine. Many wives get so caught up in winning an argument at any cost they fail to see the long-term damage they are doing to their marriages—and their families. How do you respond when you and your husband do not see eye to eye?

In the middle of an argument you can have a wonderful opportunity to reflect Christ's character by working to resolve the conflict in a way that honors your husband. When you determine to live in a manner that brings God glory, you give a correct estimation of His character to those who are watching how you live—beginning with your children. And when your life reflects God's character, He can use your example to create in your children an appetite to know Christ. (On the contrary, any hypocrisy on your part could make your children reject your faith.)

Back when I was involved in youth ministry, some of the most amazing kids I knew grew up in homes where they watched their godly mother respond in a Christlike manner to a harsh husband. Because these kids witnessed their mom's genuine faith, displayed through her difficult circumstances, they were drawn to a personal relationship with Christ as well.

Sometimes the best way to glorify God is to keep your tongue from evil (see Psalm 34:13). So the next time you and your husband begin to argue, ask God to help you stop yourself from saying words that will make matters worse. Psalm 139:4 says, "There is not a word on my tongue, but behold, O LORD, You know it altogether." So in the time it takes a quarrelsome remark to get from your mind to your tongue, the Holy Spirit can—and will—remind you not to speak it. It is your job to ask Him for help and then yield yourself in obedience to the Spirit's prompting. The more often you respond in obedience to God, the more He will transform you into a peacemaker who glorifies Him.

The next way you can respond with Christ's character is...

Take responsibility for your own contribution to the conflict. When you have a disagreement with your husband, is blaming him for the problem your natural default mode? In an attempt to be helpful to your husband, do you tend to point out his flaws? You should know that regularly blaming your husband may make him feel attacked and will likely invite a counterattack—or cause him to flee your presence.

Learn from what Jesus said: "Why do you look at the speck that is in your brother's eye, but do not notice the log that is in your own eye?"[13] Is it possible you've become so focused on your husband's shortcomings that you have failed to acknowledge your own? When you are willing to overlook your husband's offenses and honestly admit your own faults, you just might find he will begin to offer you the same grace.

Don't bring up your husband's past failures. In the heat of an argument, are you tempted to pull out the list of your husband's past infractions? For example, if he overspends on a particular item, causing you to have less money for groceries that month, do you immediately harp on every other time he has committed a similar offense? Reacting in this way will certainly build a wall of discord between the two of you.

When we were newly married, Steve was invited by a man he worked with to invest in a business. The man told Steve his investment would pay out tenfold if he gave him a certain number of dollars. Steve and I talked about the investment and decided to take a chance by throwing our money into the venture. Not long after Steve wrote the initial investment check we learned there would be no pay-out—and we would never see our money again. We were disappointed but learned a valuable lesson.

I hadn't given another thought to the bad investment until more than a decade later when my husband was teaching a marriage seminar. He recounted the story to the audience and said, "Men learn from their mistakes. And I learned a good lesson that day about get-rich-quick schemes."

Then Steve addressed the wives in the group. He said, "Rhonda has never again mentioned the loss of that money. Even though she could have thrown it in my face a number of times when we were struggling to make ends meet, she never did—never. Ladies, I cannot tell you how much you will bless your husband if you forgive and forget when he makes mistakes.

"As a result of how Rhonda responded to me in that experience, my admiration, trust, and respect for her grew tremendously. And when you do the same, I am confident your husband's trust and respect will grow for you as well."

Whenever your husband lets you down, trusting him to do better the next time communicates your commitment to reconciliation. Are you willing to do whatever it takes to daily communicate forgiveness and reconciliation to him?

Freedom from Conflict

Many wives will weep for a good marriage, but they will not roll up their sleeves to do what it takes to get there. When you draw on Christ's grace, follow His example, and put His teachings into practice, you can find freedom from impulsive, self-centered decisions that contribute to conflict. As you employ the aforementioned eight steps to making peace and determine to stop fighting with your husband, loving conflict resolution is within your grasp. And when you become a peacemaker who lives to glorify God, your Christlike character will certainly bring peace to your marriage.

From a Husband's Perspective
A Word from Steve

A woman once told me, "If I just had a different husband, everything would be okay." Have you ever made this same statement or one like it? While you might think your life would be better if you had a different husband, if there is conflict in your marriage, odds are that he is only half the problem. And since part of the responsibility for conflict lies with you, if you were to divorce your husband, you would just be dragging yourself—and your unresolved issues—into yet another relationship.

Even if you could find a man who would always let you have your way, if you never dealt with your selfishness or any of the unbiblical ways you relate to others, it would only be a matter of time before the fighting started up again.

If you're like most married couples, the conflicts in your marriage relationship come as a result of disappointment. For example, when you have a specific expectation and your husband does not measure up to it, you will become irritated, hurt, or even angry. Maybe your husband refuses to squeeze the toothpaste from the bottom of the tube (which I admit is a pet peeve of mine), even though you have repeatedly asked him to change his behavior. So how do you respond? First you start to nag him about it. Then maybe you dwell on thoughts like, *Doesn't he know how hard I work to keep the bathroom clean? He doesn't even respect all I do around here.* (I know this sounds silly, but believe me, a majority of arguments in a marriage begin at this level of disappointment.)

Maybe you don't lash out or say anything at all when you are disappointed. Instead, you just determine to keep your mouth shut—all the while mentally rehearsing in your mind what you would like to say to your husband. Keeping your mouth shut "to keep the peace" without changing your negative thinking is like putting a Band-Aid on cancer and hoping it will go away. Obviously just covering up the problem won't make it leave. You have to address the problem itself.

If you want to stop fighting with your husband, take a good, long look at yourself and bring the truth of God's Word into the ways you interact with your husband. Evaluate your contribution to your marriage conflicts, and confess your sins to God. Ask your husband to forgive you, and allow God's Word to transform you. Every one of these actions will go a long way toward bringing more peace into your marriage.

Look again at the eight principles Rhonda laid out in this chapter. Make those steps the habits of your life. Developing new habits takes continued effort. When you fail, confess it to the Lord, then do the right thing the next time. And don't give up!

Hebrews 12:14 says, "Pursue peace with all people." God has called His children to dwell in peace with one another. What more important place can you begin to live out peaceful relationships than in your own home? Discipline yourself to become a woman of peace, and soon you will find that resolving conflict God's way will become your passion. When this happens, your home will be a place where peaceful relationships are enjoyed. And without harsh conflict in the home, your children will feel more secure and will come to learn the keys to biblical conflict resolution for their own marriages.

Wives, listen to chapter 8 audio
"Too Busy to Build a No Regrets Marriage?" at
RhondaStoppe.com/marriage-mentor

Man to Man

Everyone likes to be a winner, right? You may recall how recently thousands of people paid a great deal of money to watch a fight between two popular fighters. Each had declared how they would beat senseless their opponent, yet in the end, only one made good on his threat. Only one left the ring as the victor.

While watching a professional fight might be entertaining, observing a married couple go toe to toe is anything but. Especially when children are the ones with front-row seats to the main event. In conflict, most of us would like to emerge the winner. However, you should know when conflict arises between you and your wife, winning should not be the point or purpose. The trouble with fighting to win over the one God has given you to love and protect is that it's self-defeating. Truth is, you really never win when your goal is to emerge the victor in a disagreement with your wife.

After a game, a good coach will have his players watch video replays of the game. As they watch he will instruct them to evaluate their performance on the field. This process is effective in coaching and is also an important practice for any man who wants to better himself as a husband, father, and man of God.

Take some time for a little self-evaluation. How do you react to conflict? Most likely your response to conflict is something you learned while you were growing up. If you grew up fighting till the last man was standing, you'll likely bring that behavior into your marriage. And if you were raised with "the silent treatment," this may be your default when you're faced with conflict.

In my experience, most men react to conflict in one of two ways: either you'll stay in the fray and fight it out, or look for a way to escape.

I suppose it's normal for wives to be quick thinking and faster than men to formulate their thoughts into words. Rhonda tells me it's common for a wife to have her argument all prepared in her mind before her husband even walks in at the end of the day.

Maybe that's why men feel so unprepared when they are met at the door with a barrage of "you always—you never—and you forgot to." When this happens, most men will lash out in frustration. Other men deal with conflict by walking away and going silent.

Learning to become a man who resolves conflict in a Christ-honoring way is essential to building a home of peace.

Learning to become a man who resolves conflict in a Christ-honoring way is essential to building a home of peace. All couples have conflict; it's how you interact with each other to resolve the issues that will grow your love for one another and honor Christ. Determine now before the Lord that fighting and arguing will not be the characteristic that defines your home environment, and then make every effort with God's help to keep this commitment for a peaceful home life.

From a Wife's Perspective
A Word from Rhonda

In this chapter I shared with your wife some practical ways she can learn to resolve conflict in marriage in a way that brings peace to your home and honor to Christ. Read them with her and have a discussion about practical ways to be peacemakers in your home.

Together, watch chapter 8 video at
RhondaStoppe.com/marriage-mentor

Thinking It Through

1. Write out and memorize Romans 12:18.

2. When conflict arises, do you tend to flee or attack? Consider and talk about how each of you responds to conflict. From the eight steps to becoming a peacemaker, name two specific steps you will employ to bring peace into your marriage.

3. With regard to the onset of an argument, what insight do you learn from Proverbs 15:1?

Living It Out

1. What does James 4:1-2 say is the reason for fighting and quarrels?

2. Are you so passionate about getting your way that you will fight to get it? If so, name at least one way you will let God redirect your passions to glorify Him and bring peace to your marriage.

If you grew up in a home where people fought—or if your marriage has been characterized by strife—the idea of conflict-free living may be unfamiliar to you. Remember, arguing or withdrawing to the silent treatment both represent conflict in your marriage. If in your marriage you've made it a habit to clam up and withdraw when you're hurt or angry, don't think just because you're not arguing you're not in conflict.

Working toward a peaceful home is worth the effort. It will bless your marriage and your children with a sense of security and well-being. So don't give up. Your persistence will result in progress, and God will be glorified as peace reigns in your marriage.

3. Take a moment now to pray together, asking God to help you learn how to resolve conflict biblically.

9

Our Marriage Would Be Better If Bad Things Would Stop Happening

THE JOY OF THE LORD IS YOUR STRENGTH

Several years ago Steve went on a dirt-bike camping retreat with some of the men in our church. Around four o'clock in the afternoon on the second day of their retreat, my phone rang. You know the call you get that causes your heart to sink? This was that kind of call. A friend on the other end of the line said Steve had been seriously injured in a motorcycle accident. I was told that Steve lay unable to move in a canyon where emergency personnel were having a hard time rescuing him. *Rescuing him?* I thought.

I asked, "How bad is his injury?"

My friend didn't have much information except that Steve was hurt badly and was waiting to be rescued by helicopter. She also said that it had started to snow, so Steve was in the elements and going into shock as he waited. With the promise of a phone call when she knew more, I hung up the phone. I happened to be at my brother's house when I received this disturbing call, so we all stopped to pray for Steve and his impending rescue.

171

Hours went by—and no phone call. Because there was no cell service where the men were camping, I was unable to reach any of them. Finally, about four hours later, I called my friend Denel, who said her husband, John, had just walked in the door from the camping trip. John informed us that a rescue team had just hiked Steve to the top of the canyon, where they were now airlifting him to the hospital. In the end, Steve had lain in the dirt and cold in excruciating pain for seven hours while waiting to be rescued.

Around nine o'clock that night, I finally received a call telling me which hospital Steve was be flown to. My brother then drove me the 90-minute ride to Stanford Hospital.

I was so relieved when I finally got to see Steve at the hospital that I immediately covered his face with kisses—and tears. He was pale, covered with dirt, and still had gravel in his mouth, which I immediately began to scoop out from inside his cheeks. Then I learned that Steve had shattered his right hip and would require extensive surgery. I'll spare you all the gory details of what is involved in putting a person with a shattered hip socket into traction while they await surgery, but suffice it to say, our oldest daughter, Meredith, nearly passed out.

Once Steve was admitted to the hospital and given something to dull the pain, the severity of the incident began to dawn on me. The doctors were concerned his right leg would no longer be able to function, and words like *wheelchair* and *prosthetics* were being thrown out as they showed me X-rays of Steve's injury.

My husband was fragile—*fragile*! I didn't know what to do with that. This was the man who had cut off the tip of his finger and then kept working (true story). Steve had always been the rock in our family. And no matter what went wrong, he would always say, "It's going to be okay"—and we would believe him. Now who was going to say, "It's going to be okay"—and make me believe it?

For nine days, Steve was in traction awaiting surgery. I never once went home. Over the course of those days, Steve had so many visitors the hospital staff was amazed at the party that was continually going on in his room. And the kids from our church made a mural to hang in Steve's room that told the story of his accident through their drawings—complete with helicopters, motorcycles, and blood spurting out of Pastor Steve's leg. Steve loved it!

And, of course, our own kids were by our side through the whole ordeal. We laughed, prayed, and thoroughly enjoyed one another as we were gathered around Steve's traction-extended body. Our son Brandon turned 18 the night before Steve's surgery, so we all gathered in Steve's room and sang happy birthday to Brandon. Then we prayed for the Lord to guide the surgeon's hands as he repaired Steve's hip—and make it so he would be able to walk again.

Steve's surgery went well, in spite of the excruciating pain. The Lord graciously provided Steve with one of the best—if not *the* best—orthopedic surgeons in the nation. After placing a metal plate where Steve's hip socket had once been, the surgeon did an incredible job of repairing the damage that had been caused by the accident.

After Steve was out of surgery, we all prayed together and thanked the Lord for sending us such an amazing physician. Then everyone went home—with the exception of me and our friends John and Denel.

I had encouraged John and Denel to go home too, but they had spent their own sleepless nights in the hospital when their daughter, Cassie, had had open-heart surgery, and they said they were staying. I gratefully accepted their offer. (Talk about living out 2 Corinthians 1:4—they comforted us with the comfort by which they themselves had been comforted.)

And If the Accident Wasn't Enough...

About one and a half hours after our two youngest kids had gone home, I received a phone call from our daughter Kayla, who was crying hysterically. She reported how icy and snowy it was up at our house. I immediately said, "Oh, Lord—no, not another accident!"

Kayla calmed down enough to say, "No, we are fine. It's the house. It's completely flooded with water!"

Apparently during all the time we had been spending at the hospital, the water pipes in our house had slowly filled up with ice and finally burst. Because our wood-burning stove had not been lit for a number of days, the house had become very cold. And because Steve had just filled our 5000-gallon water tank before he left on his camping trip, the entire tank had emptied into our house when the pipes burst.

Even as I tell this story here, I have to stop and take a deep breath because of the enormity of all that had happened at the time. As I sat in the hallway of the hospital hearing the news about our flooded house, all I could think of was how relieved I was that the phone call had not been about Kayla and Brandon being in an accident. I kept telling Kayla, "It's okay, honey. It's just stuff. It's going to be all right."

The nurses at the nurses' station (who had become good friends by now) were all watching me as I hung up the phone and dissolved into tears. Once I composed myself, I was able to smile and again repeat, "It's just stuff." And to the watching nurses I was able to share how I had peace from knowing my God would work all things together for good (see Romans 8:28).

I was so thankful John and Denel had stayed the night because they encouraged us while we were in shock over yet another catastrophe. It wasn't long before they even had us laughing at the "comedy of errors" the whole fiasco had been.

After the kids' call, I called my brother, who immediately drove up to our house. Then I called our church family, who by the next morning were at our house removing all of the water and saturated flooring. All the while, they lovingly ministered to our kids.

The next day a hospital administrator came to Steve's room to inform us our insurance company said we were not covered for the expenses we had incurred. After she left the room, I stood next to Steve's bed trying desperately to keep it together for his sake. Steve could see how much that bit of news was threatening to devastate me, so he beckoned me to himself. As I climbed into his bed, he pulled me up close and said, "It's gonna be okay."

With those words, I melted into Steve's chest and wept. Not just over the misunderstanding regarding our insurance (which was later resolved—praise the Lord), but also over all of the unbelievably painful events we had experienced over that ten-day period of time.

Romance comes in many forms, but one of my favorite romantic moments between Steve and me happened when he held me closely that day and whispered words of encouragement into my ear—despite the excruciating physical pain he was still feeling from his injuries.

Once we got home from the hospital, Steve's recovery was long and painful—and I never left his side. I was determined not to leave him to feel lonely or discouraged. "We're in this together, baby," I would tell him.

All through the long, sleepless nights and the sorrow I experienced while watching my sweet husband in so much pain, the Holy Spirit kept whispering to my heart, "The joy of the Lord is your strength" (Nehemiah 8:10). No, I did not hear an audible voice, but as loudly as I can describe to you as one's heart can hear God speaking, over and over again He reminded me *the joy of the Lord is your strength*. I shared this with no one, but pondered it in my heart during the darkest moments of those difficult days. Taking God's words seriously, I determined to fight for joy in spite of how difficult it was to watch my love suffer so. And all through that time we were living on concrete floors and sorting through possessions that had been ruined by the flood.

The Joy of the Lord Is Your Strength

While Steve was recovering from surgery, I was very protective over him. Well-meaning people who wanted to visit did not know how little sleep Steve was getting or how much pain he was enduring. One person in particular kept calling and asking to come up and visit with Steve. Several times I said no, but then Steve said, "Ah, let him come up. It'll be okay."

Reluctantly I said to the caller, "You can come up, but you can't stay long."

When the man arrived, I left him alone with Steve to talk. By the time they were done, Steve had led the man to the Lord! (And here I was being a protective wife when God wanted to use my husband in his weakness.)

The first Sunday that Steve and I were able to attend church, we could hardly wait to see our sweet church family, who had so blessed us with prayer, food, and continuing on in the work of the ministry while we were away.

After the service, the man who had accepted Christ in our home gave me an envelope to "encourage me," he said. Inside was a lovely card with a beautiful scripture across the front. And when I opened the card, there it was—an incredible love note to me from the Lord!

Upon a small tile placed inside of the card was inscribed, "The joy of the LORD is your strength—Nehemiah 8:10."

Just remembering that makes me cry! I hadn't told anyone about the Lord getting me through each day with those words from Nehemiah 8:10—no one! And our heavenly Father, in His kindness, sent this new believer to me with a loving note from His Word—the very words His Holy Spirit had been whispering to my heart. Grateful tears spilled from my eyes that day, just like they are now. In that moment, Psalm 139:17 washed over my heart and mind: "How precious also are Your thoughts to me, O God! How great is the sum of them!"

The same God who so gently walked us through our trials is the One who will walk with you through yours as well. How do you and your husband respond when you are going through difficult events? Are you drawn closer to one another as you look to Christ for answers? Or do you turn on one another and blame each other for the calamity?

I have a friend whose son was hit by a car and killed. He told me that after the accident, a wedge grew between him and his wife. Both were grieving, and both were blaming themselves and each other for the accident. Sadly, over time, they got divorced.

Are You Surprised by Trials?

Why is it some marriages fall apart when they go through hard times while others seem to grow stronger? Let's unpack this question, shall we?

Over the years that I have been involved in ministry, the one common response I have observed in Christians when they encounter a trial is they are often taken by surprise. This includes individuals who know that bad things happen to good people (one even wrote a book about that). But when their own little world is visited by difficulties, they are not only shocked, but they are downright bewildered. And this is often when Christians begin to question God's love for them.

The apostle Peter said that we should fully expect troubled times and warned, "Beloved, do not be surprised at the fiery trial when it comes upon you to test you, as though something strange were happening to you" (1 Peter 4:12 esv).

In that verse, the word *happening* in the phrase "as though something strange were happening to you" means "to fall by chance." One Bible teacher explains it this way: "A Christian must not think that his persecution is something that happened accidentally. God allowed it and designed it for the believer's testing, purging and cleansing."[1]

Because people tend to question God's goodness when trials come, it is important for you to understand how God allows—and even orchestrates—trials in the lives of His children to accomplish His purposes.

Four years ago when our eldest daughter gave birth to Ivy, who had unexpected birth defects, the joy of the Lord again proved to be our strength. Although our whole family was definitely surprised by and sorrowful because of the physical challenges God allowed Ivy to be born with, we were able to comfort our own hearts and each other with the remarkable knowledge of God's sovereignty and His promise to work together for good whatever He allows to pass through His loving fingers. And what an incredible joy sweet Ivy has been to our family. With each surgery and challenge she faces, her feisty, joyful little spirit delights our hearts.

If during your darkest hours you and your husband remind one another of God's goodness and encourage one another with scripture, your hearts will move toward one another as you grow closer to Christ.

In Isaiah 55:8, God says, "My thoughts are not your thoughts, nor are your ways My ways." When we learn to trust that God's ways are good regardless of how difficult our circumstances are, then our lives—and marriages—can grow stronger to reflect more clearly His glory to those around us. And if during your darkest hours you and your husband remind one another of God's goodness and encourage one another with scripture, your hearts will move toward one another as you grow closer to Christ.

First Peter 1:6 says, "In this you greatly rejoice, though now for a little while, if need be, you have been grieved." In other words, that which brought grief to you can become a reason for rejoicing.

So, wait a minute: Am I to believe that Steve's accident was not really an "accident" but something God allowed—dare I say God deemed *necessary*—for our spiritual growth?

I believe the answer is yes! Sure, the pain my husband endured was terrible. And yes, the road to healing was long and difficult. However, there's no question that God accomplished good through what had happened. And we will never fully know all the good that God did until we stand in heaven, where God will reveal to each of us all the good He did on our behalf.

All through our trial, God continually gave us the peace to endure, and He provided for our every need. And when the house was flooded, our kids discovered a deep love and willing helpfulness from our church family. They showed us God's love not only by cleaning up the house but also by generously purchasing new flooring for our home.

What's more, during Steve's time of recovery, the church was robbed and Steve's laptop—with all his sermon notes—was stolen. And the money the church had collected for our flooring turned up missing. (By this point, all we could do was laugh when yet another "trial" came into our already topsy-turvy lives.)

Through it all, the joy of the Lord truly was our strength. We and our children learned where the source of joy was during that time: the Lord Himself. In the years since, we have watched our kids and their spouses fight for joy whenever trials have visited their lives. And walking with us through our trials prepared Meredith and Jake to trust the Lord when Ivy was born. As a parent it is important to remember that sometimes the trial God allows is less about you and more about preparing your children to trust God later in life when they face their own seasons of trouble. If by example your kids observe your unwavering trust in the Lord amidst the storm, your actions will do far more to train them for the future than your words ever will.

Looking back at all the ways the Lord took care of us gives us more reason than ever to trust God in every circumstance.

Don't Look at the Waves

Most of us have heard the story of when Peter stepped out of the boat during a storm to walk on the water toward Jesus:

> Peter answered him, "Lord, if it is you, command me to come to you on the water." He said, "Come." So Peter got out of the boat and walked on the water and came to Jesus. But when he saw the wind, he was afraid, and beginning to sink he cried out, "Lord, save me." Jesus immediately reached out his hand and took hold of him, saying to him, "O you of little faith, why did you doubt?" And when they got into the boat, the wind ceased. And those in the boat worshiped him, saying, "Truly you are the Son of God" (Matthew 14:28-33 ESV).

Peter took a great step of faith when he stepped out onto the raging sea—a faith I'm not too sure I would have had. How about you? Summoning his courage, he put one foot in front of the other as the waves raged around him. That had to be very intimidating—even terrifying! But then he took his eyes off of Jesus and focused instead on the stormy wind and waters, and he began to sink. Before the waves could swallow Peter, Jesus reached out and pulled Peter to Himself—and to safety.

I know many sermons have been preached on the importance of keeping our eyes on Jesus when the storms of life come, but the message bears repeating. So let's look a little closer at this familiar story and see if we can gain a better understanding of how and why God permits trials in the lives of His followers. As we do so, I'd like for us to start by looking at the bigger picture of what happened in Matthew 14.

From the Mountaintop

Right before the disciples were caught in that terrible storm, they had just experienced the glorious miracle of Jesus feeding the 5000 with the loaves and fishes. Talk about a mountaintop experience! Top that off with the fact everyone who was fed witnessed the miracle too. That had to be incredible—wouldn't you agree?

Right after the 5000 were fed, Jesus *made* the disciples leave. Matthew 14:22 says, "Immediately Jesus made His disciples get into the boat and go before Him to the other side, while He sent the multitudes away."

Jesus knew what was next: a raging storm. But the disciples didn't, and I wonder if they were a little disappointed that they didn't have more time to bask in the glorious experience they had just been through.

Have you ever found it hard to leave a place where you saw God's hand in action? For Steve and me, youth camp was one such place. There were many times when we saw the Spirit of God convict kids and draw them to surrender to Christ. At the end of each camp, we hated having to leave because we knew how the world would try to pull those kids away from their commitments to the Lord. I recall one year in particular in which two kids who had attended camp went home to their friends who used drugs. That year, as a result of their destructive behavior, both kids passed away.

What a difficult thing it is for youth workers to see firsthand the consequence of a teen's choice to turn back to the world, away from the beckoning of the Holy Spirit. If you've never worked in youth ministry, you may be tempted to think a youth pastor's job is all fun and games, but anyone who has worked with teens (as we did for 18 years) knows the highs and lows of the ministry. Please remember to pray for and encourage your youth ministers in their unique calling. And remember, Satan would like nothing more than to destroy the marriage of your ministry leaders, so please stand in prayer for God to bless their relationships.

And if you are in a ministry marriage facing difficulty, don't be tempted to believe getting help shows weakness. Satan loves to isolate godly leaders and make them believe getting help for their marriage would somehow hurt their ministry. On the contrary, a ministry couple who is willing to seek out godly counsel shows signs of maturity and wisdom.

Steve and I can attest to the powerful impact godly counsel can have on a ministry marriage. For more than a decade we have devoted ourselves to mentoring ministry couples whose marriages are in trouble. We've seen wonderful transformation for many couples after a week of marriage mentoring with us at our ranch.

Into the Storm

Back to the account of Jesus feeding the 5000 with loaves and fishes. Why did Jesus send the disciples into the storm immediately following this glorious event? Why didn't He join the disciples in the boat?

While Jesus stayed behind to pray (Matthew 14:23), He was fully aware of the disciples' situation. In the same way, when we face trials, it can often feel like Jesus is far away. And yet Hebrews 13:5 promises that Jesus will never leave nor forsake us. Even though He may send us into a tumultuous sea, we can know Jesus is right there with us, and He is always praying for us as we toil in our specific situation (see Romans 8:34).

Maybe you've had times when it seems as though Jesus doesn't respond immediately to your pleas for help. Remember when Mary and Martha sent for Jesus to come heal their sick brother? Jesus did not come right away. Instead, He waited two whole days. And He said to the disciples, "This sickness is not unto death, but for the glory of God, that the Son of God might be glorified through it" (John 11:4).

I love how the apostle John assures the reader, "Now Jesus loved Mary and her sister [Martha]" (verse 5) before he tells us that Jesus waited two more days before going to them. Don't you sometimes feel like God doesn't love you when He doesn't rescue you in a timely manner? Satan loves to whisper in your ear, "If God really loved you, He wouldn't have allowed this to happen." Don't fall into the trap of believing this lie and walking away from the only One who can turn your trials into something beautiful for your good and His glory (Romans 8:28).

Fighting the Storm

After fighting the storm late into the night, the disciples saw Jesus walking toward them on the water. But at first they didn't recognize

Him. In fact, they thought He was a ghost and they cried out in fear (Matthew 14:25-26). Sometimes when we are in the midst of a terrible storm, we are so focused on fighting it that we don't recognize Jesus when He comes to us. And because the disciples were not expecting Jesus to rescue them, it may have never occurred to them to even watch for Him.

In the same way, do you find yourself working so hard to pay the bills, fight an illness, or heal your marriage that you are not even watching the horizon for your Savior to come and help? Maybe your eyes are fixed on your circumstances, and you are hoping that somehow, everything will work out. Are you placing your trust in yourself instead of the Lord?

Resting in God Himself

When Jesus arrived at the boat, He told the terrified disciples, "Take heart; it is I. Do not be afraid" (Matthew 14:27 ESV). Notice Jesus didn't say, "Don't be afraid; I am going to fix this situation." No, He simply said, "Guys—it's Me!" When Jesus speaks, hearts are calmed and hope is renewed.

Whenever you are going through a struggle, the best place to find courage is from our Lord Himself. Some people cry out, "God, give me a sign" or "Show me what to do," when Jesus simply wants you to focus on Him—not on how He is going to make everything better.

When the apostle Paul struggled with an infirmity and asked God three times to heal it, God responded, "My grace is sufficient for you, for My strength is made perfect in weakness" (2 Corinthians 12:9). Then Paul said, "Therefore I take pleasure in infirmities, in reproaches, in needs, in persecutions, in distresses, for Christ's sake. For when I am weak, then I am strong" (verse 10).

Only God knows the reasons He has allowed the trials you experience. And the sooner you let go of trying to figure out how to escape the trial or how to fix the problem, the sooner your faith will grow and God's peace will rule in your heart. This goes for your marriage as well. When you stop looking to your husband to resolve the problem and let him off the hook, and he sees you walking in faith through the raging sea, peace will wash over your marriage in a beautiful surge, and you will find that *the joy of the Lord is your strength.*

There's one more observation I'd like to share from Matthew 14.

Stepping Out in Faith

When Peter recognized that it was Jesus who was approaching the boat, he said, "Lord, if it is You, command me to come to You on the water." And Jesus said, "Come" (Matthew 14:28-29). I love how Peter responded here. Poor Peter often said things that got him in trouble, and even today people talk about the times when he lacked faith. But here, Peter was the only disciple who stepped out in faith when Jesus called to him. All the other guys stayed in the boat. Oh sure, they watched Peter walk on the water. Maybe they were even cheering him on. But none of them had the courage to step out and join him.

Do you have that kind of faith? When you fix your eyes on Jesus and remember that He is sovereignly in control of all of life's circumstances, you will not only weather the storms of life, but you may even find the courage to say, "Bring it on, Jesus. Call me to step out in faith. My eyes are on You."

You Are on a Mission

Every follower of Christ is called to reach people for God in their generation. We are to make Christ known so that people might come to redemption. As a Christian, anything you do in your life should be filtered through this missional statement:

> *To know Christ and make Him known.*

When you and your husband learn to live with a mission perspective, you will stop looking to each other to fix a difficult situation and turn to God instead. And you will trust that whatever trials or blessings God allows to come your way are divinely orchestrated by Him so "that you may be blameless and innocent, children of God without blemish in the midst of a crooked and twisted generation, among whom you shine as lights in the world" (Philippians 2:15 ESV). This allows God to use whatever means necessary to shine His glory through your

obedient life so that through your testimony, He can create an appetite in other people to know Christ.

To shine brightly means to use your blessings to bless others and to
always acknowledge that it is the Lord who provides—rather than taking the glory for your accomplishments. And it means walking through
painful circumstances with joy so that Christ's peace will be seen by
everyone who is watching.

All through our marriage, Steve and I have experienced great blessings and deep sorrow. I am confident the Lord has more in store for us
as we seek to serve Him and share the gospel with the people He brings
across our paths. What about your marriage?

I challenge you to stop here and take a moment to ponder the
highs and lows of your married life. Have there been times when you
felt alone in the boat on a raging sea? How did you respond? Did you
blame your husband for not making enough money or not being sym-
pathetic enough when you were hurting? Or maybe you have not yet
gone through a truly painful experience. If so, I hate to break it to you:
you will. So rather than hope that will never happen, you would do well
to begin growing your trust in the character of Christ through prayer
and studying the Bible.

It is through Scripture that God has chosen to reveal His ways to us.
So when you read God's Word, ask Him to help you know Him better
and trust Him more. Then you will be better prepared not only to survive life's storms but to actually thrive in times of trouble.

Determine to live with a missional perspective. This means daily
asking God to do those good works He planned to do through you
before the foundation of this world (see Ephesians 1:3-6; 2:10). When
you wake up each day, ask God to give you a passion to seek His face
through His Word so you can learn to trust Him more.

Will you courageously ask God to use every circumstance in your
marriage to show others that a relationship with Christ is the only
way to true happiness? Even if your husband does not keep his focus
on Christ, when you do you can joyfully build a marriage that will
grow stronger through life's blessings and sorrows—and God will be
glorified.

From a Husband's Perspective
A Word from Steve

Bad things. They always seem to happen when you least expect them, right? Your kid breaks his arm. The car overheats and breaks down at the most importune time, or an unexpected bill arises. How do you respond to these everyday occurrences? And how do you react when something much worse occurs—something that completely rocks your world?

Your knee-jerk reaction when things don't go right reveals a lot about you. Are you one who is quick to ascribe blame when the unexpected occurs? When you're blindsided with a difficult circumstance, is your natural response to think, *Whose fault is this?*

Trying to find the person whose action caused the situation is all too often the response for husbands and wives. And sadly, when one turns to blame the other, rather than finding strength from each other to walk through the trial, a wedge is driven between the couple. This wedge can cause conflict and resentment that can leave indelible scars on the relationship.

What about you? When one of the kids gets seriously hurt while dad's in charge, is your immediate response to say something like, "Why weren't you watching him more closely?" Maybe you didn't blatantly say, "This is all your fault," but questioning your husband in that way implies to him where you have assigned blame.

Most husbands know when they've messed up, even if they won't admit it. After we men make a mistake, we usually beat ourselves up pretty good. Joining in to make your husband feel worse is not the best way to draw him to you in times of crisis.

What if you really believed that long before the trial occurred, God knew about it and allowed it into your life? If you sincerely believe that the Lord's purpose for the trial is to grow your faith and bring honor to His name, do you think you might respond with a different attitude?

So, what can you do the next time a trial comes out of nowhere? Change your thinking. Determine to look at bad things from a different perspective. Refuse the temptation to ascribe fault, and ask God to help you look at the trial as an opportunity to bring honor to our Lord by your response.

The next time you're faced with a difficult situation, look for ways to build up your husband, rather than tearing him down. Here are some practical ways for you to walk through a trial:

- Tell your spouse you don't blame them.

- Keep a proper perspective. How can God use this to draw others to our Savior, beginning with your kids?

- Remember this as something the Lord has allowed.

- Look for what you can learn. How does God want you to grow from the experience?

- Evaluate your internal responses and let God change you. Trials have a way of showing us what's really going on in our hearts.

- Look for others who have gone through the same hardship. How did they properly respond? How might you follow their example to improve your outlook? (Reading biographies of godly servants of Christ is a great way to learn from others' examples.)

- Learn from others' mistakes. Discern if the person's response was godly. What did they regret? What bad consequences came from wrongly blaming their spouse or responding improperly? How can you keep from making the same mistakes?

Determine to trust Christ BEFORE the trials come. The apostle Peter said, "Beloved, do not think it strange concerning the fiery trial…as though some strange thing happened" (1 Peter 4:12). Peter was talking about persecution, but I believe you can apply this principle to your own life as well. Rather than waiting for the trial to come and then scrambling to recover from the surprise of the circumstance, take to heart Scripture's warning, and learn from the example of other godly people who have gone before you.

In my experience people whose marriages not only survive trial but grow more in love with each other amidst the struggles of life are those who have a proper perspective of how God uses trials to make them more like Christ. Couples who are grounded in God's Word *before* the trials come are best prepared not only to withstand the storm but shine as a beacon of hope to others.

> Wives, listen to chapter 9 audio "Joy Is Strength— So LOL!" at **RhondaStoppe.com/marriage-mentor**

Man to Man

Rhonda just shared with your wife how I shattered my hip in a dirt-biking accident. (If you ride dirt bikes, I hope that story doesn't freak out your wife so she never again lets you go riding with your buddies.) Here's what happened. A little over ten years ago, I went on a motorcycle camping weekend with some men from our church. My son Brandon was 18 at the time, and we were pumped to spend the weekend together riding dirt bikes.

The first day of riding was great! On the following day, Brandon and I rode into a canyon and jammed up the other side of the hill while throwing a rooster tail of dirt and rock behind us.

As I was making one last run, my front tire locked up in an unexpected rut in the road, and before I could correct it, I was thrown from my bike. My right hip crashed against the handlebar as I went over the bike. Within seconds I was on the ground in excruciating pain. At the time I had no idea that my hip had been totally shattered on impact. Yes, it was terribly painful.

Have you ever been in such great pain that death didn't look so bad? Scary, isn't it?

When bad things happen, how do you respond? Most people work their way through a variety of responses, such as sadness, anger, fear, blaming others, blaming themselves, or even blaming God. I am amazed at how often people blame God for their struggles. Even when they can look back and see that the cause of their difficult circumstance was their own doing, many people continue to blame God for the consequences of their own poor choices.

I have no doubt my poor judgment was the cause of my accident, but I am equally convinced the Lord allowed the trial to bring about His good in my life and the lives of those around me. Can you think of a time your poor choices brought about painful circumstances? In those times, how did you react? How you respond in times of trouble reveals a lot about your heart and your level of trust in God.

Did your last trial put a wedge between you and your wife or did it draw you closer together as you looked to Christ for comfort?

When you find yourself in the middle of an unexpected trial, is your automatic reflex to blame your wife or others around you? Maybe you're even tempted to blame God. What would happen if, instead, you began to develop a habit of looking to Jesus? With your eyes fixed on Him—rather than the trial—you will find His peace and hope even if your circumstance doesn't change.

My accident put me in traction for nine days and left me with permanent damage to my sciatic nerve, causing chronic pain and affecting the way I now walk. And while I was in the hospital, the pipes in our house burst and our 5000-gallon water tank spilled out into our home. With all the unexpected events happening, I had a choice to make: *How am I going to respond?* While it wasn't easy, every day, every sleepless night, I wrestled against discouragement and looked to the Lord as my source of strength and even joy.

When you learn to look for what good God might accomplish through the hardship you are facing, you will discover how to glorify Him in the trial. When you suffer, God can be glorified in a number of ways:

- God will show Himself powerful on your behalf by rescuing you from the pain.

- God will grow your trust in Him to prepare you for an even greater trial to come.

- God will draw others to know Christ because of the faithfulness they observe in you.

- Fellow believers will be encouraged as they observe your joyful trust and commitment to Christ.

The faith of your children can increase greatly
when they see you and your wife determine
to trust Christ through difficult times.

- The faith of your children can increase greatly when they see you and your wife determine to trust Christ through difficult times.

Jesus warned His disciples, "These things I have spoken to you, that in Me you may have peace. In the world you will have tribulation; but be of good cheer, I have overcome the world" (John 16:33). I love that Jesus gave His followers—and us—this assurance so that we can face life's trials with His peace.

And Jesus' words should help you realize that nothing surprises God. Every struggle, heartbreak, and disappointment is filtered through His loving hand. Remember that as a Christian, you are on a mission to shine brightly the hope of Christ to a world who desperately needs Him. Any blessings or struggles you experience are opportunities for the Lord to redeem the lost, encourage fellow believers, and mold you and your spouse more into the image of His Son. Living with this perspective will enable you to build a marriage that not only withstands the storms of life but also holds out hope to those the Lord brings into your path.

From a Wife's Perspective
A Word from Rhonda

When Steve got injured and our house flooded with water, I remember trying to keep it together for his sake and for our kids. But I can honestly say every moment of every day of that season I had to fight to not be overcome by the "what-ifs" and "if onlys." The day Steve pulled me into his hospital bed and just held me while I cried brought more courage to me than just about any words he could have spoken at that time.

If you are in the midst of a storm, remember that putting your strong arms around your wife may be just what she needs to find the strength to face another day. When she sees you keeping your eyes on Jesus while the waves crash around you, she will be filled with a sense of security that you will guide her through the trial with God's strength and peace. And remember, often the trial is part of God's plan to make you both more like His Son and examples to your children (if you have them) of how to look to Jesus as their source of joy and strength when one day they themselves face uncertain times.

Together, watch chapter 9 video at
RhondaStoppe.com/marriage-mentor

Thinking It Through
---

1. Learning from others' experiences is a great way to prepare yourself to withstand the storms of life. In the Bible God has provided us with many examples of people who trusted in the Lord while facing unthinkable struggles. Take some time to look up these accounts and talk about how God used their trials for their good and His glory.

   David: 1 Samuel 17 (pay specific attention to verses 34-37) —

   Joseph: Genesis 39–41 (notice Joseph's perspective in Genesis 50:20) —

   Heroes of the Faith: Hebrews 11 —

After you are done, spend some time together in prayer. Ask God to help you live like these heroes of the faith. Pray that you will remember you are on a mission to hold out the hope of salvation to a generation in desperate need of Jesus. And remember how Christ shines brightest when His children walk in His peace amidst the inevitable storms of life.

If you find yourselves now in a storm, here are some scriptures to help you navigate through the storm.

   2 Chronicles 20:12 —

Hebrews 12:2—

2 Corinthians 4:7-9—

2. Read Psalm 119:25-32, then make a list of actions you should take when your soul is "covered with dust."

--------------------- **Living It Out** ---------------------

Talk about why you think looking to Jesus during a trial will help your marriage grow stronger. In the section "From a Husband's Perspective," Steve shared with wives some good habits you can develop in preparation for the next time you find yourself facing one of life's storms. Those steps bear repeating, so we are including them here:

- Evaluate your internal responses and let God change you.
- Look for others who have gone through the same hardship.
- Learn from others' mistakes.

Take some time to review and talk over the steps below together and talk about how you might implement these practical responses the next time you're blindsided with a trial (or perhaps you can apply them now if you find yourselves facing a storm at this time).

- Tell your spouse you don't blame them.
- Keep a proper perspective.
- Remember this as something the Lord has allowed.

- Look for what you can learn.
- Evaluate your internal responses and let God change you.
- Look for others who have gone through the same hardship.
- Learn from others' mistakes.

Photo credit: JPlazaPhotography

10

Hope to Be Happy

DETERMINE TO ENJOY YOUR SPOUSE

From the time Jim and Elizabeth George first met, they fell in love. Elizabeth says, "Ours was truly love at first sight as we passed and smiled at each other regularly on our way to and from classes."[1]

"It was a bright autumn day at the University of Oklahoma. As I hurried toward my first class after lunch, I noticed him again. He was smiling as he came my way…Well, evidently he noticed me, too, because soon [in November] a mutual friend set up a blind date for us."[2]

On Valentine's Day, Jim asked Elizabeth to be his bride. And by June, 22-year-old Jim and 20-year-old Elizabeth were married. Of their courtship, Elizabeth says, "There was never a dull moment, and fun was the center of all we did…Wow, what a whirlwind of excitement!"[3]

Of their honeymoon, she adds, "Truly, it seemed like we were standing on the threshold of a lifetime of joy, love, excitement, and passion…This is how our wonderful friendship and marriage all began."[4]

After the honeymoon, however, it didn't take long for reality to set in. Elizabeth was working full-time, and Jim worked long hours with a one-hour commute each way to his job. With life's demands weighing heavily on their marriage, Jim and Elizabeth focused on the work in front of them.

Elizabeth remembers, "Things went well for a while. And then…

both Jim and I would tell you that after eight years, things became awfully empty and got pretty rocky."[5] She says,

> We fumbled, we argued, and we let each other down. Because we didn't find fulfillment in our marriage we poured our lives into causes, friends, hobbies, and intellectual pursuits. Having two children also didn't fill the emptiness we each felt. Our married life droned on for eight frustrating years until, by an act of God's grace, we became a Christian family…Giving our lives to Jesus Christ made a tremendous difference inside our hearts.[6]

Becoming a Christian did not change overnight the habits that had been established in their marriage. As time went on and they learned to apply the Bible's truths to their relationship, theirs became a happy marriage. And they have since written a number of books in which they share what they have learned about God's design for marriage.

In her book *A Wife After God's Own Heart*, Elizabeth offers this valuable insight:

> Your commitment to follow God's plan for a wife makes a tremendous difference. How? It will make a difference in the atmosphere in your home, in your communication as a couple, in your heart as love for your husband blossoms and abounds, and in the way you treat him with great respect. It will also improve the climate of your marriage, paving the way for the two of you to dwell together in harmony.[7]

In addition, Elizabeth strongly recommends that wives make sure to keep the fun in their marriage. One morning some years ago, Jim added the word *fun* to Elizabeth's daily planner to playfully remind her to include some downtime in their busy schedules. She says, "If Jim and I aren't careful, we can give ourselves to all work and no play! So just as we learned to persevere at our work and in the upkeep of our home, we have learned (and are still learning!) to remember to have some fun along the way."[8]

Can You Relate?

Can you relate to Jim and Elizabeth's experiences? I can. Before the wedding, did you dream of how much fun it would be to be married? Setting up house and caring for your man were likely welcome tasks on your list. But when the life you imagined doesn't happen, disappointment is sure to set in.

If you find yourself in the middle of an unfulfilling or even difficult marriage, do not despair. Jim and Elizabeth turned their marriage around, and with God's help, so can you. Let's find out what is involved in making that happen.

DECIDE TO ENJOY YOUR SPOUSE

> Some of the best marriages are enjoyed by couples who make the time and effort to playfully delight in one another.

Some of the best marriages are enjoyed by couples who make the time and effort to playfully delight in one another. Right now, can you think of a couple whose joy is contagious? Don't you just love to spend time with them? Don't you long to *be* them? What can you do to become more like the couple you desire to emulate?

First off, think back to a time when it was downright fun to spend time with your man. How did you enjoy one another back when you were dating? You didn't fold your arms, tap your foot, and say, "Okay, I'm here. Now make me happy." No—more than likely, you *planned to have a good time* simply because you were happy to be with your love.

With all the distractions life throws at you each day, you have to *decide daily* to enjoy your spouse. And when you determine each day to celebrate the time you spend with your husband, you have taken an important step toward making your marriage a delight.

I remember a brief conversation my parents had when I was 17 years old. My father, who had the day off and was working in the garage, came into the house and said to my mother, "Hey, I need to run to the store to buy a ladder. Wanna come?" Without even looking up from washing the dishes, my mom replied, "Why would I want to go with you to buy a ladder? That's not fun."

I watched my dad's face fall and shoulders shrug as he walked back out to the garage. My mom was completely oblivious to how her response had dashed my father's hopes for a fun trip to the store. However, the incident made an indelible impression on me.

When you are looking for ways to enjoy your husband, even running the simplest of errands together can provide an opportunity for some fun. When our kids were young, Steve and I would wait until the little ones had gone to bed, and then leaving them in the care of their older sister, we would sneak off to a 24-hour home improvement store. Steve was doing yet another remodel of our home, so there were frequent purchases to be made. This meant we had little money to spend on dates, and less time than usual for Steve to devote to me.

So I had a choice to make. I could have insisted Steve do all the shopping himself and complained that he never had money or time to spend with me. Or I could go with him to the home improvement store and find ways to enjoy an otherwise arduous task. Remembering how my mother missed an opportunity to have fun with my dad, I chose to go with Steve.

Even now I am smiling as I remember those late-night runs. We were surprised to discover the store played some pretty amazing music late at night. Steve and I actually danced in the aisles when our favorite '70s songs played.

Celebrating Your Anniversary at a Biker Bar?

Some years ago when we were still raising our kids, Steve's parents lived near us in a home on our ranch because his mom suffered from Alzheimer's disease. At this time, we were also remodeling our one-bedroom house. As our wedding anniversary approached, Steve and I talked about going out on a date to celebrate.

Since Steve's father was dealing with his wife's illness, and we didn't have any babysitters living nearby, we resigned ourselves to not being able to go out. However, the more we acquiesced to the possibility of not celebrating, the more determined I became to figure out a way to have our date. In the end, we put our younger two children to bed and left our 11-year-old daughter with the telephone in her hand on speed dial to her grandfather, who lived next door.

Steve and I drove five minutes up the road to a little biker bar—the only eatery within an hour of our home out in the country. Sitting at the bar, we ordered burgers and fries. It didn't take long before we both were laughing long and hard at our circumstances. I remember saying, "Here I am, a city girl, excited for an anniversary date with her man at a remote biker bar."

Because I chose not to sulk or complain about our circumstances, we had a wonderful evening. And do you know what I found out? First, the place where we ate makes an amazing burger—and the fries were out of this world. Second, we were both reminded that the reason we got married was because we truly enjoyed spending time together—no matter what we were doing. Even if it meant celebrating our anniversary by playing pinball at a biker bar in the middle of nowhere.

Have you forgotten how to enjoy your husband? When your idea of a perfect evening cannot be met, do you sulk or complain? Have you noticed that when you grumble it drives your husband away from you?

The Bible says, "It is better to live in a corner of a roof than in a house shared with a contentious woman" (Proverbs 21:9 NASB). Get the picture? Complaining about how disappointed you are when you can't have your way will not make your husband want to spend time with you. On the contrary, as this proverb points out, your contention will drive him away from you—maybe to the garage, to longer hours at work, or even to the very corner of the housetop!

Husbands are energized by a joyful wife. When you learn to become a person your husband enjoys spending time with, you may discover him looking for more opportunities to refresh himself with your company.

There Is Hope

If you are reading this and thinking, *That's me! I am not a happy person. No wonder my husband doesn't enjoy spending time with me,* well, there is hope! The first step to becoming a joyful wife is to realize you can change.

Are you ready to make some changes? To help make the following points easy to remember, let's use the word *HOPE* as an acrostic:

Hate the sin.

Open your eyes.

Pray for God's help.

Enjoy your husband.

Hate the Sin

Take an honest look at the kind of wife you have become. Do you think your husband would say you are fun to be with? If your husband seems to look for reasons not to be with you, could it be because he doesn't enjoy your company? If so, it is time to face up to your part in what is lacking in your relationship. No matter how much you may be able to assign fault to your husband, will you courageously ask the Lord to help you see *your* sin in the situation? Then ask God to help you be ruthless with your sin so you hate it and its destructive consequences as much as God does. Colossians 3:5 says, "Put to death… what is earthly in you" (ESV).

Open Your Eyes

Stop placing all blame on your husband and take responsibility for what you can do to build a happy marriage. Jesus said, "Why do you look at the speck in your brother's eye, but do not consider the plank in your own eye?…Hypocrite! First remove the plank from your own eye, and then you will see clearly to remove the speck from your brother's eye."[9]

Human nature seeks to blame others for our unhappy circumstances. So if you are blaming your husband for the lack of pleasure you find in your marriage, you should know Jesus calls you to evaluate your own sin before you criticize your husband's shortcomings.

One Bible teacher says, "Most people feel free to judge other people harshly because they erroneously think they are somehow superior…Other people are not under us, and to think so is to have the wrong view of them…The wretched and gross sin that is always blind to its own sinfulness is self-righteousness…The very nature of self-righteousness is to justify self and condemn others."[10]

Do you have a self-righteous attitude toward your husband? Have you developed a habit of blaming him for your unhappiness? Won't you open your eyes to your own sin? Once the plank is removed from your eye, then you can see yourself, God, and others more clearly. And only then will you be in the right mind-set to humbly take steps toward making your marriage a more enjoyable union.

In this age, happy marriages are rare. People often ask my husband and me, "What's your secret to a happy marriage?" This question provides us with a wonderful opportunity to tell them about Christ. Steve and I are careful to share how God is the source of our happiness and that through His Son, they too can experience true joy.

One of the most dynamic evangelistic
resources you have at your disposal is a happy
marriage that reflects the joy of the Lord.

One of the most dynamic evangelistic resources you have at your disposal is a happy marriage that reflects the joy of the Lord. And the first place you as a couple should share the gospel is to your own children. Sadly, many children raised in Christian homes reject Christ because of their parents' unhappy marriage. When you and your husband are not in unison, not only will you lack joy, but others will be negatively influenced as well—especially your children. However, when you and your husband are enjoying one another, your joy will spill over to all of your other relationships—including those with your children. "Your decision to live in obedience to God will reverberate righteousness in generations to follow…how glorious it will be for you to look back at your life and see the godly influence your actions had upon your children and grandchildren."[11]

Pray for God's Help

About her own attempt to change her unlikable ways, Elizabeth George says she learned to pray at the first hint of frustration or self-pity. She also advises wives to pray three times a day for their husbands.

Doing this will help you draw closer to your husband and get to know him and his needs better, and most important of all, love him as God does.

While there are many books written on the topic of prayer, might I suggest you just take time to pray? One tip I can share is that when I learned to talk out loud to the Lord, my prayer life became much more personal. Here is a prayer I have prayed for my husband for more than 30 years:

> Lord, cause me to love my husband with Your selfless love. Help me not to keep a record of wrongs and to forgive quickly. Give me Your joy in my marriage and Your peace in my home. Help my husband to have eyes for me only, and grow his love for me ever stronger by the power of Your Spirit.

Enjoy Your Husband

When your husband tells you about his day or recounts a story, stop what you are doing and look him in the eye. Lean toward him as he talks. Smile, nod, and laugh when it's appropriate to do so. Don't make him work to get a response or chuckle out of you. Remember how any attempt he made to be funny while you were dating was met with your laughter? How about you bless him with that kind of attention again?

Determine to be his girlfriend. One way to do this is to simply sit with him while he works on a project. Not to criticize or to add your two cents, but to enjoy watching him work. And if your husband asks you to go with him to the hardware store, drop everything and go with him. You never know—you may find yourselves dancing in the aisle to music at midnight.

Realizing your husband is not the source of your happiness and learning to find joy in your relationship with Christ are the keys to a happy marriage. Elizabeth George determined to be a wife after God's own heart, and it transformed her marriage. When you do the same, there is H-O-P-E for your marriage as well.

From a Husband's Perspective
A Word from Steve

In this chapter Rhonda talked about how Elizabeth George grew to be a wife after God's own heart by determining to grow in her walk with Christ. So I thought it would be good to take a moment to share from the perspective of Elizabeth's husband, Jim. In his book *A Husband After God's Own Heart*, Jim says:

> I would like to report that my spiritual growth, which started when I was just six years old, was a magnificent upward spiral, and that it had few, if any, valleys. But no. Sad to say, my spiritual growth in those early years was an up-and-down roller coaster. And the downward drop on that roller coaster continued into my early adult life and had a serious effect on my marriage...
>
> Spiritual growth is the key to all that is important in life. That's what Jesus meant 2000 years ago when He told a listening audience not to be anxious about life and living. He said, "Do not worry, saying, 'What shall we eat?' or 'What shall we wear?'" (Matthew 6:31). These things are definitely needful, but they are not what's really important. They are not your first priority. What's really important is your spiritual growth.[12]
>
> It's true that spiritual growth takes terrific effort. But, my friend, it's also true that the rewards are great...No matter how old you are or how long—or short!—you've been married, the day you accelerate your growth in the Lord is the day your marriage is positively impacted, improved, and strengthened![13]

No matter how your marriage has gotten off track, in my experience when one or both in a couple begins to practice the above steps, their love for one another grows, their marriage is transformed, and their relationship glorifies Christ. When this happens, it brings the light of hope to a generation who longs to believe that a relationship with Jesus really is the answer to all of life's struggles.

Wives, listen to chapter 10 audio "The Secret to Happiness" at **RhondaStoppe.com/marriage-mentor**

Man to Man

When you got married, I'm pretty sure you expected to enjoy a happy marriage. How's it going now? Would you say your marriage is a happy one? If not, don't lose heart. I have seen God help countless couples build a happy marriage once they determined to enjoy their spouse and got serious about doing the work it takes to do so. It seems strange to say you have to work to have a happy marriage, but ask anyone who has enjoyed a long and happy marriage and they'll tell you happy marriages don't just happen; they take hard work and resolve. But if you do the hard work in the beginning, you will be rewarded with years of joyful harmony with your spouse.

It's easy to get so focused on just trying to survive our busy lives that we men forget to enjoy our spouse. When you were dating, what did you do to have fun? Now that you're married, what effort do you make to have fun with each other? If you don't make time for playful interaction with your wife, you're missing an important aspect of building a happy marriage.

In this season of our lives, Rhonda and I take trips on our motorcycle. Last summer, to escape the heat we took a ride from California's Central Valley to Seattle, Washington, where we then caught a cruise ship to Alaska. I know Rhonda has learned to enjoy riding on the back of my motorcycle because it's what I really like to do. So I thought rewarding her with a nice cruise was the least I could do. (When we had little ones at home, we didn't have the freedom or finances to take such exciting trips. Even now, on a pastor's budget we've learned to look for last-minute deals.)

When our motorcycle broke down on the way home, Rhonda and I had a choice to make: we could either let this mishap ruin the rest of our trip, or we could choose to laugh and have a lighthearted attitude as we worked together to try and resolve the motorcycle's engine trouble.

Work to Have Fun

You might ask, "How do I influence the happiness in our home?" Realize that happiness does not rely on how good your circumstances are. Rather, being a happy person is really a decision of your mind. Determine to be the guy who looks at life with a lighthearted view rather than allowing the stresses of life to overtake you. When you dwell on the cares of this life, you actually allow that mind-set to steal your joy—which will make you an unhappy person. And that unhappy outlook will have a profound effect on the mood of your home.

You know how after a day of work, you play over in your mind some stress at the office or something that went wrong on the job. It's easy to get stuck there, right? Rather than dwelling on the stresses of the day, as you're on your way home, ask God to help you take your thoughts captive.

Ask yourself, "Do I have a deep-seated motivation to live this way?" If you do not, take time to consider if you have a true relationship with Christ. Philippians 2:13 says, "It is God who works in you both to will and to do His good pleasure." This means your relationship with Christ will not only make you *want* to be a man characterized by happiness in Christ, but also God promises to empower you to live in this joyful manner. If you are relying on yourself to build a happy life, you will eventually fail because the real change comes when God gives you a new heart in a relationship with Christ.

Rhonda and I have discovered that the key to a happy marriage is found in spiritual growth. And I know the same will be true for you and your marriage.

When I use the phrase *spiritual growth*, please understand I am not encouraging you to be more religious. Jesus urged His followers to love the Lord their God with all of their being (Mark 12:30). When your love for God becomes the single most important goal of your life, then prayer, reading your Bible, walking in obedience to His Word, and loving your wife will all become natural outpourings of your love for Christ.

As you devote yourself to spiritual growth, you will find lasting joy because you will learn to think biblically about your marriage relationship and life's circumstances. Will you commit to making whatever sacrifices are necessary to grow in your walk with Christ? The result will be for your blessing and God's glory, and your marriage will shine a bright light of hope to a generation who desperately needs to know that following Christ is the only answer to all of life's problems—and the source of a happy marriage.

From a Wife's Perspective
A Word from Rhonda

Is your marriage a happy one? At our No Regrets Marriage Conference, when Steve or I ask this question, we observe some of the husbands attempting to hide their disappointment while wives lower their eyes, wipe away a tear, and struggle not to show how hurt they are that their marriage is not as happy as they had expected it to be on the day they said, "I do."

For believers, our ultimate goal in life is not happiness for happiness' sake. However, God does want you and your wife to enjoy one another. Do you realize a happy marriage is a dynamic resource for sharing the gospel—beginning with your own children?

In more than 18 years of youth ministry, Steve and I have watched couples with happy marriages draw their children to the Lord. And sadly, we also have seen kids whose parents claimed to be Christians walk away from Christ because of the hypocrisy they observed in their parents' unhappy marriage.

With God's help, when you and your wife do all you can to make time to enjoy one another and build a happy marriage, your joyful testimony of God's goodness can reverberate not only to your kids but to their children as well.

Together, watch chapter 10 video at
RhondaStoppe.com/marriage-mentor

Thinking It Through

1. Discuss what hope you find from the following verses:

   Philippians 2:13 —

   1 Peter 2:9 —

   2 Peter 1:3 —

2. Are you devoted to spiritual growth? Take a few moments now to ask yourself these questions and read the following scriptures:

   - How genuine is my love for God (Mark 12:30)?
   - Am I daily adjusting my life to the precepts I learn in Scripture (Psalm 119:1-8)?

- Do I walk in obedience to Christ because of how much I love Him (John 3:36)?
- Or do I practice a religion with no real love for Jesus (Mark 7:6)?
- Am I in awe of Jesus as I discover His character through Bible study (Hebrews 1)?
- What steps can I take to make growing in my love for Christ a top priority (Psalm 119:9-16)?

Living It Out

---

1. Would your spouse say you are fun to be with? What are some ways you can make your times together more enjoyable?

2. Have you been blaming your spouse for your lack of joy? Who alone should be your source of joy?

Write out a sort of marriage bucket list of things you would like to do together. Don't argue over why you cannot afford to do the things on your list; just be extravagant and write out your "Fun Wish List."

Now make a list of some everyday fun things you'd like to do with each other as a couple and with your family. Then make an effort to actually do some of the things on your list.

11

Happily-Ever-After Is a fairy Tale

TEN KEYS TO A MORE FULFILLING MARRIAGE

D o you ever wonder what Peter's wife was thinking on the day her husband came home to announce he would be leaving the family fishing business to follow Jesus? Would this woman, who is unnamed in Scripture, have questioned Peter's decision to forsake all he had worked for to follow the One he believed was the Messiah? The Bible doesn't give us any insight into how Peter's conversion affected his marriage, but you can be sure that when I get to heaven I plan to find Peter's wife and ask her for the details of their story.

What very little we do know about Peter's wife includes the fact that Jesus healed her mother (Peter's mother-in-law) from a serious fever. Luke 4:39 tells us that "He stood over her and rebuked the fever, and it left her. And immediately she arose and served them." We aren't told if Peter's wife witnessed this healing, but if she did, I would think this would have persuaded her to get behind her husband's decision to devote his life to following Jesus.

As we'll see in a moment, history reports that Peter's wife was a courageous follower of Jesus until her final breath. This dynamic couple must have been a powerful influence for the gospel at a time when

Nero was persecuting Christians. At one point, when Peter was commanded to stop talking about Jesus, he responded, "We cannot but speak the things which we have seen and heard."[1]

The commitment of Peter and his wife to boldly proclaim what they witnessed of Jesus' life, death, burial, and glorious resurrection would eventually cost them their lives. Eusebius, a well-learned Roman historian who lived from about AD 260 to 340, made this observation about the final moments between the apostle Peter and his beloved wife:

> The blessed Peter, seeing his own wife led away to execution, was delighted, on account of her calling and return to her country, and that he cried to her in a consolatory and encouraging voice, addressing her by name: "Oh thou, remember the Lord!" Such was the marriage of these blessed ones.[2]

Can you imagine the final moment between Peter and his wife? How their eyes must have communicated volumes to each other as she was marched toward her execution? What courage she must have received to hear her sweet husband proclaim, "Remember the Lord!" as she was escorted along the path to her death. Did Peter's words remind her that in a few moments the Lord would be waiting to receive her into His kingdom?

Happily-Ever-After?

Peter and his wife were a powerful testimony for Christ to their generation. Do you realize the Lord wants to use you and your mate as a testimony to people as well? Have you ever considered that God brought you together with your husband because He has a mission for the two of you to accomplish—together?

Sadly, many Christian couples become so focused on themselves or their personal pursuits that they never reach their full potential in this life. Sure, they may work to raise good kids, pay their bills, and go to church, but in all of these pursuits it is easy to become preoccupied with the things of earth. Jesus wants us to stop focusing so much on our own comforts and happiness and instead to store up treasures in heaven, "where neither moth nor rust destroys."[3]

Can you imagine how glorious it will be to one day stand before
the Lord shoulder to shoulder with the people you and your husband
have led to Christ? I long for that day! I simply cannot wait to stand
next to Steve and celebrate with him over the many people we will
meet in heaven who came to know Jesus because God allowed us to
share the gospel with them. I don't care if we never get to retire, buy a
motor home, and travel the world. Nothing will compare to the day
we realize how every sacrifice, every prayer, and every tear was worth
all that God had planned to do through us before the foundation of
this world (see Ephesians 1:4; 2:10). And God has plans for you and
your husband as well.

For some, the story of Peter and his wife's final days would seem to
end in tragedy. But for those who realize we are all sojourners in this
life, their story really does end happily. For when they breathed their
final breath, they found themselves together in the presence of the Lord
rejoicing over the fruit of their labors—fruit that will abide forever.[4]

Ten Keys to a More Fulfilling Marriage

Throughout this book we have visited a number of myths wives
tend to believe about marriage. And the key truth affirmed in every
chapter is that true happiness is not to be found in your relationship
with your husband, but in your relationship with Christ. Let's bring
it all together now and review ten key principles to a more fulfilling
marriage:

1. Your Husband Was Never Meant to Be Your Happily-Ever-After

Asking your husband to be the source of your happiness is an unfair
expectation. You were created to delight in Christ and to be consumed
by your love for Him.

> When Christ invades your life, what spills over is a passion
> for Him and for His kingdom purposes…Your willing-
> ness to lay aside anything that besets your passionate pur-
> suit of Christ and His leading will not only set an example
> for [others] to follow, but create an appetite in [them] to do

the same…you must be set on fire by the single most glorious purpose of life—to know Christ and joyfully exhibit His greatness in *all* areas of life![5]

When you resolve to pursue loving Christ with all of your being, you will find the secret to happiness lies in your relationship with God alone. Only then can you enjoy fellowship with your husband in a way that honors Christ and blesses your husband.

2. Respecting Your Husband Will Inspire Him to Love You More

God created your husband with a deep longing to be respected by you. Just as deeply as you long to be loved without condition, your husband desires to receive unconditional respect from you. Notice I said *unconditional* respect. This means you don't get to hold hostage your respect for your husband when you aren't happy with him. Ephesians 5:33 says, "Let the wife see that she respects her husband" (esv). This is not a suggestion; this is the Lord's command to us as wives.

When you believe in your husband, rely on him, and celebrate his accomplishments, you are meeting one of his deepest emotional needs. As much as you value your husband's efforts to treat you in a loving manner, he will be grateful for your effort to treat him with honor. And when you do, don't be surprised if your husband responds to you in a more loving manner.

Your respect can motivate your husband to accomplish great achievements, because a man who is honored by his wife can do great things!

3. Staying in Love Is All About Your Love for God

Before you were married, when you fell in love with your man, you had positive and loving thoughts about him. In marriage, you must work to continue to think such thoughts about him. The Bible provides a wonderful formula that can be applied to how you think of your husband:

> Whatever is true, whatever is honorable, whatever is just, whatever is pure, whatever is lovely, whatever is commendable, if there is any excellence, if there is anything worthy

of praise, think about these things. What you have learned and received and heard and seen in me—practice these things, and the God of peace will be with you (Philippians 4:8-9 esv).

If you have not made a habit of thinking the best about your husband, you will need to determine to take "every thought into captivity to the obedience of Christ."[6] With God's help, you can gain victory over negative thoughts about your husband and replace them with thoughts that are honorable, lovely, and commendable. In our many years of biblical marriage counseling, Steve and I have seen relationships transformed when wives committed to thinking well of their husbands.

> I am confident that pursuing intimacy with God was
> the single most important influence in transforming
> my marriage, and that can be true for you too.

I am confident that pursuing intimacy with God was the single most important influence in transforming my marriage, and that can be true for you too. When your love for God is right, He will help you love your husband.

4. Parenting as One Brings Unity into Your Marriage and Security to Your Kids

Your children's security lies in the health of your marriage relationship. When you learn to live with your sights set upon God's calling on your life—to know Christ and make Him known—this will influence how you live at home. God intends for you to live in a manner that draws your kids to Christ.

Remember that your genuine love for the Lord—no matter how happy or trying your marriage may be—will do far more to draw your kids to Christ than any words you can ever say to them. Whatever trials you and your husband encounter, if your children see the two of you united in purpose to display Jesus' character in your home, they will experience security. Isn't that your desire?

Remember, your kids will be most secure when they observe their parents united, so don't disagree with your husband in front of your children about certain rules or disciplines he may impose. Determine to bow together united in prayer, rather than stand in conflict with one another, because "the effective, fervent prayer of a righteous man avails much" (James 5:16).

5. The Grass Is Not Greener on the Other Side of the Fence

Because of sin, you and I struggle with self-worship. And when you are in a state of self-love, if you're not satisfied with how your husband treats you, you may fall for the myth that you would be happier with someone other than your husband. When you find yourself toying with that idea, you can know that Satan—who comes to steal, kill, and destroy (see John 10:10)—is seeking to ruin you and your family.

When your marriage relationship fails to satisfy your longings, you would be wise to remember that no relationship can fill the void that only God Himself can fill. Realizing it is wrong to receive your sense of worth from your husband is the first step to setting him free from the burden of trying to give you what only God can give. And when you determine to find your worth in Christ, you will no longer need others to fill the void only Jesus can satisfy.

6. The Secret to Keeping Your Husband's Attention Is Finding Your Worth in Christ

What's the secret to keeping your husband's attention? While there are many points I could make to answer this question, I prefer to revisit a statement my husband, Steve, made in chapter 6 of this book:

> The secret to capturing your husband's attention for a lifetime is in learning to find your worth in your relationship with Christ. When you spend your life developing your inner beauty and staying focused on the Lord, your husband's affection for you will grow as he observes the lovely woman of God you are becoming. The more consistently you pursue Christ, the more beautiful you will become to your husband, to others, and most importantly, to Christ.

7. Pursuing Your Husband Sexually Will Fill Him with a Sense of Well-Being

Don't make your husband apologize for wanting to have sex with you. Pursue him sexually, and you will have a profound influence upon him in all areas of his life. When you make your husband feel sexually desirable, he will feel loved for who he is. You will fill him with a sense of well-being, confidence, and overall satisfaction with life.

God has given you a ministry of affirming your husband's deepest emotional needs through sex. In the same way that you long for your husband to romance you with his words and acts of love, he desires to be romanced by you through sexual intimacy.

When you happily take your husband to bed, you not only satisfy his God-given physical need for sex, but you bring healing to his weary soul as well. [7]

8. Be a Peacemaker in Your Marriage Relationship

The only way to build a marriage free of hurtful discord is through biblical conflict resolution. Make yourself so familiar with the steps we walked through in chapter 8 that the next time you and your husband begin to argue, you can stop yourself from fighting and instead take time to reflect on how you can show Christ's character. By working to resolve conflict in a way that honors your husband, you can begin to live in a manner that reflects the Lord's character to those who are watching how you live—beginning with your children.

When this happens, your home will be marked by peace. Your children will feel more secure, and the peacemaking habits you practice in your home will, in turn, train your kids how to make peace in their relationships—including their future marriages.

9. The Joy of the Lord Is Your Strength

Life is filled with blessings and struggles. Learning to see each experience as an opportunity for the Lord to shine His light through you is the first step to realizing God has a purpose in whatever He allows to come your way—even a difficult marriage.

When you choose joy in each experience you encounter, you can become a vessel for the Lord to reach the lost and encourage others—as well as mold you, your husband, and your children more into the image of Christ. When you live with this perspective, you will discover the secret to living above life's circumstances and the joy of the Lord will indeed be your strength.

10. Live with a Missional Perspective

Remember that God's goal for your marriage is for it to shine brightly the love of Christ so that He might draw others to know His Son. While it is easy to get distracted by the cares of this life, remember: financial success, comfort, and entertainment are not the path to a happy marriage.

Looking to Jesus, the author and finisher of your faith and growing in your love for the Lord through Bible study, prayer, and fellowship with other Christians who live with a missional perspective are the key to selflessly loving your spouse. And faithfully practicing these disciplines will help you live with an eternal perspective that will bring reward not only in your marriage and the security of your children but also one day when you hear from our Father, "Well done, good and faithful servant."

> Wives, listen to chapter 11 audio "The Apostle Peter's Love Story" at **RhondaStoppe.com/marriage-mentor**

Fairy-Tale Life

We wish we could sit down with you together as a couple to mentor you one last time as we wrap up this book. But since that isn't possible, in this final section we are going to attempt to chat with you as a couple. Imagine if you and your spouse are meeting with Rhonda and me in our office over a nice cup of coffee.

Steve: I'm not going to sugarcoat it for you. God never intended this life to be an easy road where you skip along having all your hopes, dreams, and aspirations met. In fact, if looking for a life of ease has become your habit and characterizes your goal for existence, it's time to reevaluate what your life purpose really should be. Our culture definitely teaches that finding true love will be the source of true happiness. And sadly, all too often when people live under this belief, they blame their spouse when they can't seem to be happy.

Rather than hoping for your wife to measure up to your expectations so you can enjoy a happy marriage, what would it be like if you were to focus less on your spouse's responsibility for your sense of well-being and you looked more at God's goal for your life?

God's goal for your life is to bring honor and glory to our Lord in *everything* you do. Look at Jesus' example. All through His ministry on earth He repeatedly stated His job was to do the will of the Father. This included speaking only the words of the Father and living daily to bring glory to God—rather than glorify Himself.

Glorify means living in a manner that reflects God's character. Husband, the Bible instructs you to love your wife as Christ loves His church. If how Jesus loves His bride—the church—is to be the standard for how you love your wife, does the way you conduct your life and interact with your spouse line up with His example of selfless love?

And, wife, lest you feel left out. Are you loving your husband in a way that shows him honor so as to build him up rather than tear him down? Take a minute to ponder how your love measures up to how God wants you to love your husband. Does the way you love your husband glorify Christ and shine brightly the testimony of His Spirit in you? Remember, His light shines brightest when times are hard. Learning to draw near to God and to your spouse in both good and bad seasons will honor your husband and shine as a light to a generation who is looking for hope. You have this hope if you are a Christian.

To be a true follower of Jesus Christ is not just adding belief in Jesus to your life. Rather, true Christians are called to deny themselves. That means laying down your own pursuits, passions, and entitlement mentality to take up your cross and follow Christ. You may think forsaking everything to live for God's purpose for your life is a tall order for God to put on His children, and you're right; it really is. But Jesus promised His yoke is easy and His burden is light (Matthew 11:30).

Living a life surrendered to Christ will allow His Spirit to work powerfully through you, and living in this way is the true evidence of a genuine Christ follower.

If you really do not care about living a life surrendered to Christ, let me along with the apostle Paul encourage you to, "Examine yourselves as to whether you are in the faith" (2 Corinthians 13:5).

Rhonda: Remember the rich young ruler who came to Jesus? He acknowledged who Jesus was but was unwilling to sell all his earthly possessions to follow Christ (see Matthew 19:16-30). Does that mean God wants you to sell everything to prove your love for Him? Not necessarily. But He does want you to live more concerned with what He wants to accomplish through you during your time on earth than on how you can store up more stuff to make yourself feel happy, accomplished, and comfortable.

Thirty years ago, when Steve and I ended up selling most of our stuff to move to our little house in the country to live without power and sleep on a sofa bed for two years, did I cry? You bet I did. *Lots* of tears. But even when everything in me longed for the comfortable life we left behind, the Lord impressed upon my heart that as high as the heavens are above the earth, so God's ways are above ours (see Isaiah 55:9). Because I had memorized this scripture years before, the Lord used it to comfort my heart and cause me to trust His ways, even when I endured the discomfort He called us to for that season. (Did I mention I slept on a sofa bed in the living room for my entire pregnancy with our last child? Talk about discomfort!)

Steve: You may have heard the tongue-in-cheek adage, "He who dies with the most stuff wins." The truth is, "He who dies with the most stuff *still dies*." And the only ones who "win" are those who have stored up treasures in heaven by living in a manner worthy of their calling (see Matthew 6:20; Ephesians 4:1).

Jesus said His followers will be evident by their lifestyle of believing and obeying His words. As it relates to your marriage, rather than focusing so much on how much you think you deserve to be happy in this life, look to how God can use you in whatever your circumstance and season of life to shine His glory in this generation.

Finish Well

Rhonda: Recently Steve and I had the honor of meeting Dr. James Dobson. For 40 years, through his books and radio programs, Dr. Dobson's ministry has helped countless marriages and families (including our own).

When Dr. Dobson asked Steve, "After three decades in ministry, what is the one thing that weighs most on your heart?"

Steve's eyes welled up with tears as he responded without hesitation, "I want to finish well."

Dr. Dobson reached over and grasped Steve's arm and tearfully responded, "Me too...me too."

No matter what season of life you're in or what you've accomplished in the past, realize the importance of living with the unwavering resolve to finish well. This generation needs the hope of the gospel and godly mentors to guide them toward lives well lived. If you've been married for a number of years, it's time to strengthen your marriage so you are ready to mentor other couples toward marriages that honor Christ.

I am so thankful for the older couples God brought to mentor Steve and me when we were newly married. They were so in love, so committed to staying in love and growing their love no matter what circumstances they faced in life. That kind of love is contagious. And seeing them live it out in front of us gave us hope that we too could grow more in love with each passing year. And these days we are learning from some of these same couples how to grieve as God takes home before them the love of their life. Even in their sorrow, the joy of the Lord is their strength and God is being glorified. What a legacy, right?

It kills me how often middle-aged couples end up getting a divorce after years of "staying together for the sake of the kids." This has never been God's intent for marriage. If you ever are tempted to think your kids would be better off if Mom and Dad separated, you're wrong—dead wrong! In our 18 years of youth ministry, we repeatedly watched children be devastated by their parents' divorce. Don't think your kids would be any different.

I'd also like to add that in the many years Steve and I have ministered, I can't tell you how many times people who divorced said, "Please warn people not to rush to divorce. I never should have left my first marriage. I was blinded by my belief that I was entitled to be treated in a way that made me feel good about myself. I am dealing with the same problems in my next marriage and now realize the issues I struggled with in marriage number one might have been resolved with maturity and good counselors. I just didn't give it a chance. I deeply regret that divorce has brought pain and havoc upon my children."

Steve and I are convinced that you will find hope and help for a happy marriage if you put into practice the biblical principles we have laid out in this book. These truths have not only been the light to our own path for a joyful marriage, but they have helped guide countless couples toward a marriage without regrets.

Will You Be That Couple?

Determine, with God's help, to draw near to Christ and one another amidst life's triumphs and trials.

Steve: Oh, my brother or sister, this is what God is calling you to. Life goes through seasons, some happy, some sad, and some just really hard. But realize this is life for all of us. Determine, with God's help, to draw near to Christ and one another amidst life's triumphs and trials. Even when you're in a season of status quo, don't forget to live with your sights on Christ and eternity. This focus will not only get you through, but it will help you live above life's circumstances to find true joy and peace in your marriage and in all aspects of life. Even if only one of you is willing to change, God can bless your marriage with peace.

Please don't ever let the words slip through your lips: "God freed me of this relationship and now I am happier than ever before." As a pastor I cringe whenever I hear someone make such a statement. (Of course, I'm not talking here about marriages in which there has been abuse.) God is more interested in your holy life than in your happiness. Does that statement make your cringe? Our culture has been so engrained in the belief that happiness is the ultimate goal in life that it's often a hard pill to swallow when someone suggests otherwise. I get it, but stay with me here.

Choosing to obey God's command to keep your covenant to your spouse will bring more blessing to you than pursuing momentary happiness, which is a fleeting emotion. Because when you purpose to live a life that honors and obeys Christ, God promises to be with you and to work all things together for your good and His glory (see Romans 8:28).

As you work to put into practice all you have learned in this book, don't grow discouraged if your marriage doesn't change overnight. Resolve to keep working at it. God is the One who can help you and your spouse change. And if your spouse doesn't seem to be making any effort, rather than growing resentful—which will steal your joy and render your prayers ineffective—choose to forgive them. Then you can pray powerfully for God to do a work in their heart. Rhonda and I have observed countless marriages transform when spouses stop undermining and manipulating each other, but instead determine to adjust their lives to truth and rely on God for help.

Rhonda: Resolve to finish well by loving God with all of your being, loving your spouse with His selfless love, and keeping your eyes on Jesus. Trust Christ to complete the work He has begun in you and your relationship, and you will enjoy a no-regrets marriage.

Together, watch chapter 11 video at
RhondaStoppe.com/marriage-mentor

Thinking It Through

Spend some time praying over the "Ten Keys to a More Fulfilling Marriage." List here, or in a notebook, what steps you feel most compelled to apply to your marriage. Discuss with each other some ways you can adjust your lives to what you have learned in this book.

Living It Out
---

1. Commit to reviewing what you've learned in this book by choosing to do one or more of the following:

   • Over the next 12 months, review one chapter each month and ask the Lord to show you how He would have you continue growing in your love for Him and for your spouse.

   • Using the principles in this book, mentor another Christian couple (or start a small group or online study group and go through the book together).

   • Give a copy of this book as a resource to share the gospel with a non-Christian couple in need of marriage help.

   • Buy a copy of this book for a Christian couple engaged to be married.

2. Pray, pray, and pray some more for God to transform you through His Word. Ask Him to give you His perfect love for your husband, and pray for Him to make your marriage one that shines brightly the message that Christ is the answer to every need.

But Wait There's More!

It's easy to be inspired by a book but then file it away as another Christian self-help book in your library. However, we would like to encourage you to make a dedicated effort to apply the truths you learned in this book daily. We are confident doing so will change you and your marriage because these truths are based on the life-transforming Word of God.

So please keep this book nearby, review it from time to time, recommend it to your friends, host a book club to mentor other couples toward a no-regrets marriage, and walk engaged couples and newlyweds through these pages. God will do more than you can imagine through your obedience in becoming a godly mentor to the next generation.

And since financial stress is one of the main causes of marital conflict, we've written a bonus chapter to address this issue of finances in marriage. *To learn how to obtain a copy, visit* RhondaStoppe.com/marriage-mentor.

Photo credit: JPlazaPhotography

Photo credit: Eric McFarland Photography

Appendix:

How to Have a Relationship with Jesus

W hat on earth could she possibly mean by a *relationship* with Jesus?" you ask. I am so glad you want to know!

Did you know that God created people so that He could have a relationship with them? When the Lord created Adam and Eve and put them in the garden of Eden, He did not leave them there with a list of religious rituals to perform while He observed from afar. No, Genesis 3:8 says that God walked with Adam and Eve in the garden in the cool of the day. He spent time with them!

You have likely heard some form of the story of how God put a tree in the garden and commanded Adam and Eve not to eat of its fruit or they would surely die (Genesis 2:17). Genesis chapter 3 records how one day Satan came and tempted Eve to partake of the forbidden fruit. Eve was deceived and seduced by Satan's lies and ate the fruit—and of course Adam followed suit. In the moment that they disobeyed God's command, not only did their bodies begin to die physically, but what's worse is that they died spiritually. Can you imagine how empty they must have felt when that happened?

You see, once Adam and Eve sinned, they had rejected God's rule and yielded themselves to Satan. And without someone to rescue them, they were without hope of ever being in right standing with God again.

Because of their rebellion against God, they could no longer fellowship with Him, for God cannot allow sin in His presence. And unless God provided a way that Adam and Eve—and by extension, all of mankind—could have that relationship restored, they would forever be without hope. Every one of us was destined to spend eternity in hell, separated from God's presence.

However, because of God's great love for His creation, He had planned a way to rescue us and bring us back to Himself (that's why we use the word *salvation*!).

Revelation 13:8 says that Jesus was "slain from the foundation of the world." That means even before God created the world or people, He knew that all of us would need a Savior. And because of His great love for us, and His desire to have a people who would *choose* to love and serve Him, He put the tree in the garden to give Adam and Eve a choice. When they sinned (and He knew they would), God told them that He would offer up His Son to pay the price for their disobedience (see Romans 5:12-21).

Imagine—God loved us so much that He sacrificed His only Son, that whoever believes in Him will not die but will live forever (John 3:16)! God says the very act of offering His greatest treasure, Jesus, was His way of showing you and me just how very much He loves us. "God demonstrates His own love toward us, in that while we were still sinners, Christ died for us" (Romans 5:8). What an amazing way for Him to show us how much He loves us, huh?

So what does it mean to believe in Him like John 3:16 says? Is it a mere mental assent to the truth that Jesus is fully God and, being fully God, He took on the form of a man when He was born through a virgin? And that Jesus lived a sinless life and willingly gave Himself up to die a cruel death on a cross, and then He victoriously rose from the dead so that His blood could wash away our sins and He could give us eternal life? While all of those statements are true, if you simply *agree* with the facts about Jesus, that does not mean you have a *relationship* with Him. In fact, James 2:19 says even the demons believe, and they tremble in fear because they *know* who Jesus is and what He accomplished when He died for our sins.

No, having a relationship with Jesus is entering into a personal covenant (that's a big word that means "vow" or "promise") with Jesus. He wants us to make a lifelong commitment to Him—but how?

First, God wants you to repent of your sins (*repent* means to agree with God that you are a sinner in need of a Savior and that you will turn away from your sins). The Bible says, "All have sinned and fall short of the glory of God" (Romans 3:23). Only the blood of Jesus can wash away your sins (Hebrews 9:14).

I know it's easy to take offense when someone says, "You're a sinner," but let's be honest: you and I both know that even though we try to do what's right, our natural instinct is to disobey God's laws.

You see, God gave us those laws *not* so that we could try to become sinless by doing all that they command, but to show us that we will *never* be able to measure up to the sinless life God requires of us to have a relationship with Him and enter into heaven when we die (see Galatians 2:16; 3:24).

So where does that leave us? If Galatians 2:16 says that no man is justified by the works of the law, then how can we possibly be restored to God and go to heaven? If God isn't making sure our good deeds outweigh our bad deeds by the time we die (a completely bogus concept not taught in Scripture), and if, as Romans 6:23 says, "the wages of sin is death," how can we be rescued from judgment?

I'm glad you asked! For the Bible also says, "The gift of God is eternal life in Christ Jesus our Lord" and that we are justified (made right) "by faith in Jesus Christ" (Romans 6:23; Galatians 2:16).

The Bible teaches that Jesus is not simply one of many ways to salvation; He is the *only* way. In John 14:6, Jesus said, "I am the way, the truth, and the life. No one comes to the Father except through Me." Those are Jesus' words, not mine. The *only* way to an intimate relationship with God is through Jesus. It is only when you receive His free gift of salvation that Jesus' blood washes away all of your sins. God Himself says, "Though your sins are like scarlet, they shall be as white as snow" (Isaiah 1:18).

Think of it—God promises to wipe the slate completely clean! No matter how many bad decisions you have made up to this point, no matter how shameful your past, Jesus is offering you freedom from all of it! Freedom from shame and the bondage of sin.

Once Jesus washes away your sins, He promises *never* to throw them in your face again. The Bible says, "As far as the east is from the west" is how far God removes our sins from us (Psalm 103:12). (You do realize that east and west never meet, right? That means that in Christ, our sins are taken away *forever*!)

But you don't get to just say some magic words, "I believe," and then go back to life as usual. Jesus says He wants you to surrender all that you are to Him. "If you confess with your mouth the Lord Jesus and believe in your heart that God has raised Him from the dead, you will be saved" (Romans 10:9-10).

Jesus doesn't ask you to simply add Him on to your life. He wants to *be* your life. And to anyone who becomes Jesus' follower, He promises that He will give you a new and pure heart. Second Corinthians 5:17 says, "Old things have passed away; behold, all things have become new."

Believe me when I tell you that without a relationship with Jesus, I was a selfish, arrogant, fearful, and materialistic woman. But when I accepted Jesus' free gift of salvation and surrendered my life to Him as my Lord, I was set free. I have never looked back! Jesus took the mess that I was and gave me a new heart. Through Jesus, God forgave all of my sins—*all* of them! And when I said yes to entering into a relationship (there's that word again) with Jesus, He put within me His Holy Spirit. (So that's what was missing!) And God wants the same for you.

When God fills you with His Spirit, life makes sense! In fact, it's the life you were born to live, in fellowship with your Creator. Nothing else in this life will ever satisfy your longing for Him—nothing.

If you enter into a relationship with Jesus, you never have to worry about being "good enough" for God to love you or let you into heaven when you die. To those who are in Christ, God says He adopts us as His very own children. "Behold what manner of love the Father has bestowed on us, that we should be called children of God!" (1 John 3:1). Jesus says we can call God, "Abba, Father" (that means "Daddy"—Romans 8:15). And God says His great love for us is perfect, immeasurable, and nothing we could ever do will make Him stop loving us (see Romans 8:35-39)! To top it off, God promises you will never be alone again. Jesus promises He will never leave you nor forsake you (Matthew 28:19-20; Hebrews 13:5). How awesome is that?

And there's one more thing: if you decide to believe that Jesus died for you, and you choose to agree with God that you are in need of a Savior because of your sinful heart, and if you pray and submit to Jesus as the Lord of your life, then God's Spirit will fill your heart with His presence, peace, and purpose.

When you receive Jesus' free gift of salvation, He promises to lead you, guide you, and accomplish great things for His kingdom through you for the rest of your life. Ephesians 2:8-10 says, "By grace [that means you can't earn it] you have been saved through faith, and that not of yourselves; it is the gift of God, not of works, lest anyone should boast. For [you] are His workmanship, created in Christ Jesus for good works, which God prepared beforehand." God has a plan for your life. Isn't that exciting?

So now you know what it means to have a relationship with Jesus. It is my prayer that the Holy Spirit is drawing you to Christ even at this moment, and that you will pray to receive Jesus as your Lord and Savior so that you can begin this wonderful journey of walking with Him for the rest of your life, and on into heaven in the next!

> To watch a video of Rhonda sharing How to Have a
> Relationship with Jesus, visit **NoRegretsWoman.com**

Notes

Chapter 2: What's the Big Deal About Respect?

1. Rhonda Stoppe, *Real Life Romance* (Eugene, OR: Harvest House Publishers, 2018), 92-93.
2. Dr. Emerson Eggerichs, *Love and Respect* (Nashville, TN: Thomas Nelson, 2004), 15.
3. Eggerichs, 87-89.
4. Eggerichs, 89.
5. To learn more about the *Love and Respect* book and conferences, visit Dr. Eggerichs at Loveand Respect.com.

Chapter 3: We're Falling Out of Love

1. Luke 6:36.
2. Shaunti Feldhahn, *For Women Only* (Sisters, OR: Multnomah, 2004), 166, 169.

Chapter 4: Your Marriage Can Survive Toddlers and Teenagers

1. John MacArthur, *Twelve Extraordinary Women* (Nashville, TN: Thomas Nelson, 2005), 92.
2. MacArthur, 95.
3. Francis and Lisa Chan, *You and Me Forever* (San Francisco, CA: Claire Love Publishing, 2014), 163.
4. James 5:16 (ESV).
5. The name of the Bible study that Steve referred to is *Experiencing God* by Henry Blackaby (Nashville, TN: B&H, 1998).
6. Blended families can find help at FamilyLifeToday.com/resources/blended-families/.

Chapter 5: The Grass Is Not Greener on the Other Side

1. Paul David Tripp, *What Did You Expect?* (Wheaton, IL: Crossway, 2010), 210.
2. Dr. Emerson Eggerichs, *Love and Respect* Video Conference, Colorado Springs, Focus on the Family (2004).
3. 1 Peter 5:8; John 10:10.
4. Tripp, 196.

Chapter 6: Telling Her She's Pretty and Keeping His Attention

1. Janet and Geoff Benge, *George Müller, the Guardian of Bristol's Orphans* (Seattle, WA: YWAM Publishing, 1999), 43.
2. Benge, 75-76.

3. Benge, 79-80.

4. Song of Solomon 1:8.

5. Julie Gorman, *What I Wish My Mother Had Told Me About Men* (Franklin, TN: Authentic Publishers, 2013), 25.

6. Genesis 3:11-12.

7. Jeremiah 17:9.

8. Elyse Fitzpatrick, *Idols of the Heart* (Phillipsburg, NJ: P&R Publishing, 2001), 130, 132.

9. Hebrews 4:12.

10. Psalm 139:23-24.

11. Jerry Bridges, *The Pursuit of Holiness* (Colorado Springs, CO: NavPress, 1986), 78.

12. Shaunti Feldhahn, *For Women Only* (Sisters, OR: Multnomah, 2004), 166, 169, italics in original.

13. Ruth 2:9.

14. *The MacArthur Study Bible* (Nashville, TN: Thomas Nelson, 1997), 373.

15. Ruth 1:15-18; Proverbs 31:10-12,23.

16. Ruth 1:16-17.

17. 2 Peter 3:18.

18. Ruth 2:2,7,17,23; Proverbs 31:13-21,24,27.

19. Ruth 2:12.

20. Proverbs 31:11.

21. Rhonda Stoppe, *Moms Raising Sons to Be Men* (Eugene, OR: Harvest House, 2013), 180; quote originally from Arnold Dallimore, *Spurgeon, A New Biography* (Carlisle, PA: The Banner of Truth Trust, 2005), 36.

22. Ruth 2:7; Proverbs 31:26.

23. 1 Corinthians 13:5.

Chapter 7: All He Wants Is Sex

1. John MacArthur, *Daily Readings from the Life of Christ* (Chicago, IL: Moody, 2008), 184.

2. Shaunti Feldhahn, *For Women Only* (Sisters, OR: Multnomah, 2004), 94.

3. Feldhahn, 99, 101-2.

4. Feldhahn, 99.

5. Feldhahn, 139.

6. To find out more about biblical counseling and counselors near you, go to the website for the Association of Certified Biblical Counselors at http://www.biblicalcounseling.com.

Chapter 8: Every Couple Fights

1. Julie Gorman, *What I Wish My Mother Had Told Me About Men* (Franklin, TN: Authentic Publishers, 2013), 63.

2. Gorman, 65.

3. Gorman, 120.

4. Jerry Bridges, *The Pursuit of Holiness* (Colorado Springs, CO: NavPress, 1986), 104.

5. *The MacArthur Study Bible* (Nashville, TN: Thomas Nelson, 1997), study note for Genesis 3:16.

6. If you suffer side effects from PMS, consider going to a doctor who specializes in hormonal issues.

7. Philippians 4:4-7 (ESV).

8. Proverbs 15:17 (ESV).

9. John MacArthur, *Daily Readings from the Life of Christ* (Chicago, IL: Moody, 2008), 78.

10. To find out more about biblical counseling and counselors near you, go to the website for the Association of Certified Biblical Counselors at http://www.biblicalcounseling.com.

11. Matthew 5:9.

12. Ken Sande, *The Peacemaker* (Grand Rapids, MI: Baker, 2004), 11.

13. Luke 6:41 (NASB).

Chapter 9: Our Marriage Would Be Better If Bad Things Would Stop Happening

1. *The MacArthur Study Bible* (Nashville, TN: Thomas Nelson, 1997), study note for 1 Peter 4:12.

Chapter 10: Hope to Be Happy

1. Elizabeth George, *A Wife After God's Own Heart* (Eugene, OR: Harvest House, 2004), 14.

2. Elizabeth George, *A Woman After God's Own Heart* (Eugene, OR: Harvest House, 1997), 57.

3. George, 162, 14.

4. George, 43, 162.

5. George, 14.

6. George, 58.

7. George, 37.

8. George, 171.

9. Matthew 7:3-5.

10. John MacArthur, *Daily Readings from the Life of Christ* (Chicago, IL: Moody, 2008), 177-79.

11. Rhonda Stoppe, *Moms Raising Sons to Be Men* (Eugene, OR: Harvest House, 2013), 71.

12. Jim George, *A Husband After God's Own Heart* (Eugene, OR: Harvest House, 2004), 9-11.

13. Jim George, 10.

Chapter 11: Happily-Ever-After Is a Fairy Tale

1. Acts 4:20.

2. Eusebius Pamphilus, *Eusebius' Ecclesiastical History* (Grand Rapids, MI: Baker, 1974), 115-16.

3. Matthew 6:20.

4. John 15:16.

5. Rhonda Stoppe, *Moms Raising Sons to Be Men* (Eugene, OR: Harvest House, 2013), 188.

6. 2 Corinthians 10:5.

7. Rhonda Stoppe, *A Christian Woman's Guide to Great Sex in Marriage*, www.NoRegretsWoman.com.

Let's Not Say Good-bye!

Keep in touch with Steve and Rhonda through social media. For regular articles, free marriage-help resources, and links to hear Steve and Rhonda on the radio, sign up for their newsletter at NoRegretsWoman.com, "like" Rhonda's Facebook page, *Rhonda Stoppe No Regrets Woman*, and follow us on Instagram and twitter @RhondaStoppe.

You can help us help other couples build a no-regrets marriage by sharing quotes from the book in your social media. When you share, please hashtag #RhondaStoppe #MarriageMentor in the comment so we can interact with you and hear about what God is teaching you. (And if you tag Rhonda Stoppe in a picture of you holding this book, we will send you a copy of the bonus chapter on finances for *free*!)

To invite Steve and Rhonda to present their No Regrets Marriage Conference at your church, or to have Rhonda come speak at your next women's event, please visit: NoRegretsWoman.com.

To learn more about Harvest House books and
to read sample chapters, visit our website:

www.harvesthousepublishers.com

HARVEST HOUSE PUBLISHERS
EUGENE, OREGON